THE MOBIUS GUIDES
spells and rituals

THE MOBIUS GUIDES

spells and rituals

TERESA MOOREY

First published in Great Britain in 2003 by Hodder and Stoughton
A division of Hodder Headline

A Mobius paperback

10 9 8 7 6 5 4 3 2 1

A CIP catalogue record for this title is
available from the British Library

ISBN 0 34082799 8

Typeset in Fairfield Light by
Palimpsest Book Production Limited, Polmont, Stirlingshire
Printed and bound in Great Britain by Mackays of Chatham plc,
Chatham, Kent

Hodder and Stoughton
A division of Hodder Headline
338 Euston Road
London NW1 3BH

acknowledgements

Many thanks to James Hunt for some interesting men's rituals, and to Graham and Margaret Matthews for their lovely Baby Dedication Ritual. Thank you to Lionel Snell for inspiration and clarification of some of my ideas. Renewed thanks to Patrick Corbett.

Thanks as always to Jane for her Gift Ritual, for always being there to talk and discuss, and for her beautiful illustrations.

contents

introduction

Prologue I

. . . Faint crescents of light glimmered at the base of her blind-fold and her nose was itching. She knew she could slip the loose bonds that fastened her wrists to the back of the chair if she so wished, but it felt important not to do this. So she twisted her head and rubbed her nose on her shoulder. The itch was almost gone, leaving room for her other discomforts. The cold air crept under the door and beneath her thin robe, peppering her flesh with goosebumps, and the seat of her chair felt like granite. There was the faintest scent of incense and she strained her ears at distant murmurs. How much longer would they be?

The anxious, uncomfortable part of her mind surveyed the other part that was held in amniotic timelessness. She might have been there ten minutes or several hours. It was still a surprise when the door opened and light surged beneath her blindfold. Warm hands loosed her bonds and helped her to her feet, removed her blindfold and guided her into the candlelight and welcome of the circle. Her robe was undone and she stood naked before friends who were also awesome strangers. Vapours of frankincense, sandalwood and a bitter undertone of myrrh breathed upon her skin, as a blunt point trembled against her breast.

'O you who stand on the threshold, have you now the courage and the will to enter?'

'I have.' She was surprised at the steadiness of her own voice. 'Then you are welcome, in the name of the Lady, and the Lord and all of us gathered here.'

Firmly but tenderly, hands at her waist directed her towards the altar, where stood figures of the Goddess and Her consort, the Horned God of Nature, flanked by large candles. All around the altar were garlands and leaves, and the pentagram glowed in the centre as if lit by inner fires. Then she was guided to her right, to face the eastern candle.

'Hear us, O powers of the East, Eurius, Powers of Air, as we present to you Grainne, witch and priestess.'

And now another quarter-circle to the right, more swathes of incense and the shuffling of bare feet behind her, as the others moved their places.

'Hear us, O powers of the South, Notus, Powers of Fire.'

And so to the West, and Zephyrus, and back to the North again, facing the altar, and the realms of Boreas, the element of Earth. A bell sounded twelve times and soft lips kissed the five magical spots on her body. Fingers dipped in oil and in wine followed the lips, and then the kisses again, sealing the matter.

'I consecrate you with my lips, priestess and witch. And I present to you the athame, the wand, the pentacle and the censer . . .' Billows of incense lifted her spirit and for a moment it was as if she hung suspended above the circle, looking down at candles that were points of light, and the heads of her friends, with their arms crossed over their chests, like folded wings.

'. . . Hear ye the words of the Star Goddess . . . I, who am the beauty of the green earth and the white moon among the stars, and the mystery of the waters, and the desire within the human heart, call unto thy soul. Arise and come unto me, for I am the soul of Nature who gives life to the universe. From me all things proceed and unto me all things must return; and before my face, beloved of gods and men, let thine innermost divine self be enfolded in the rapture of the infinite . . . And thou who thinkest to seek for me, know thy seeking and yearning shall avail thee *not, unless thou knowest the mystery; that if that which thou seekest thou findest not within thee, thou wilt never find it without thee. For behold I have been with thee from the beginning and I am that which is attained at the end of desire.'*

Again the bell was rung, and everyone came up, by turns to kiss her and embrace her. Cakes and wine were brought from the altar and passed around the circle. All were now sitting on the floor, in a relaxation and intimacy that comes only with communal nakedness. Her old robe was bundled up and thrown into the grate, where it was burnt, as a sign of the ending of her old life and the start of her new one, as priestess and representative of the Goddess, an initiate of the Old Religion. It was the end of the ceremony, but it was also, for her, a beginning.

She drunk deep of her wine, which tasted heavy and fragrant with the incense.

'I feel as if I've come home,' she said . . .

Prologue II

As she rounded the corner the wind whipped into her face. She screwed up her eyes against it and against that feeling, that familiar doubt that was stealing up on her from some shadowy place inside. No, she said, almost out loud, not again, not today. No.

The bus stop was only fifty yards away and her bus was due. She couldn't be late again. She wouldn't think about it, she'd go on, get on the bus, go off to work and not worry. But what if . . . ? No.

She was nearly at the stop and she looked at her watch. Five minutes to spare. Perhaps there was just time to . . . She felt herself slowing up. But she wasn't going to think about it. She was sure this time. Everything was okay and she was going to work, normally and sensibly.

But was she certain? It seemed as if a grinning clown's face popped up before her mind's eye, the Teaser, the Trickster. You can't ever be sure you know. What if? What then? Oh dear, dear,

3

dear. You can't just go and leave it, you know. Just think, just suppose. Ha, ha, ha. Silly girl, naughty girl.

Panic overwhelmed her and the fight was lost. Again. Caught between fear and despair, she stopped for a moment. Then she turned, pulled her coat around her and ran back to the house. She would probably miss her bus, but it was no use. She just had to go back and check. She flew down her road with the wind behind her, fumbling in her handbag for her keys as she ran. She fell against her door — yes, it had been locked all along. But what about the kitchen taps? In her haste she dropped her keys, picked them up with a handful of leaves, couldn't get the right key in the lock . . . Then she was in the kitchen, twisting at the dry tap, to make sure it was off, really off. She turned to the cooker. Yes, the gas knobs were off too. She looked closely and then looked away, then back again, three times. That meant they really were turned off, didn't it? Now she could go. Ah, but what about upstairs? Dropping her handbag she raced up, two steps at a time, into the bathroom, to strain at those taps too. Fine, now she could go, she was sure this time. Down the stairs she hopped, grabbed at keys and handbag and leapt outside, pulling the door closed behind her.

Not so fast. Lean against it, check it. She came back up the path and pushed at the door, which did not give way. It was securely locked. Check it again . . . and again. It has to be three times. Okay, now I really can go.

Her lungs burned as she ran into the wind, the wind which brought the sound of the bus engines to her ears. She rounded the corner just in time to see the bus disappear up the hill. No point in running any more. Defeated, she trudged to the stop, letting the wind blow back her coat, cooling her down. It would be twenty minutes before the next bus, and so she would be late again. She'd have to make up another excuse, and tomorrow she'd just have to get up earlier, to make room in her life for this business. Why couldn't she just go to work, simply, like everyone else? What unlabelled anxiety demanded this of her? She knew, she just knew, she had turned everything off, checked it all, closed *the door properly, and yet somehow she could not rest, or trust herself. It was as if she was paying some nameless dues by this pointless compulsion to run back and check three times – and why THREE?*

It was a ritual, a stupid ritual, that's all. How could she get free of it?

Comments

The two accounts given above illustrate rituals at opposite ends of the spectrum. The first story is one of initiation, a powerful, complex and atmospheric ritual, purposely constructed to mark an important change in the life, the assumption of new responsibility, the ending of an old state and the start of a new one and a profoundly spiritual experience. The woman concerned is purposely and consciously making a commitment to the Old Religion of the worship of Nature, to the Great Mother Goddess with her consort the Horned God. This 'religion' which is a spiritual path without any dogma except 'Harm none' is also known as paganism, witchcraft or Wicca. Every part of the ritual is constructed to have special meaning and it is poetically beautiful.

Contrast this with the second ritual. Here there is little that is conscious. Instead of awe we have fear, instead of poetry we have ugliness. There is no choice and little recognition of purpose. The ritual seems to rise up and 'grab' the unfortunate girl, who wishes only to be free of it, to be 'ordinary' and 'normal'.

What do these rituals have in common? Most notably, what they share is the ability to effect a change in consciousness. In the first example, the change is sought as a means to spiritual progress. This ritual draws the participant closer to her spiritual source, reinforces her bonds with her companions, gives her inner strength, enhances her view of life and its processes. It is essentially a very positive and joyful occasion. In the second example, a change of consciousness is also brought about, but there is no joy, only a passing relief and a feeling of bondage. The woman *knows* she has turned off all the taps, closed the door, etc., but she is unable to progress through her day without this ritual to free her from anxiety. To be 'psychological' we may say that the woman is a neurotic who is a prey to general fears due to an insecure childhood. These fears alight at points in her life, irrationally. We might say that she isn't 'really' afraid of her house blowing up, being flooded or burgled, but more generally afraid of life and an unfriendly cosmos. The rituals arise from her subconscious as an attempt to control the situation.

We might wonder whether, in the absence of 'religious' ritual, which is designed to connect us with cosmic reality, we become prey to the sort of alienation and fears that are the lot of the second woman. She wants to be 'normal' which probably means that, like most people in the Western world, she wants to exist solely in what we call our ordinary, day-to-day life, ignoring anything else as slightly cranky, but she can't. We might say she is 'unbalanced' but depression, powerlessness and meaninglessness are all too common. The first woman is wiser. She seeks meanings consciously and uses ritual as a powerful tool. This is what we shall be seeking in the following pages, in ways large and small, for by no means all rituals are complex ceremonies like the first example. We can make ritual conscious and useful, an effective tool to ease our passage and to help bring about positive changes in our lives.

1

the basics
of ritual

Custom without reason is but ancient error.

Sixteenth-century proverb

What is ritual?

'Ritual' means a set of actions, often repeated, as a ceremony or a habit. It actually signifies two main types of activity. First, it can mean ceremonial, a contrived action designed for an occasion, such as a church service or a parade. Second, it can mean an empty, repetitive schedule that we perform because we feel we must, because we have suspended our intelligence in favour of habits. The second meaning has become more prevalent, as general tastes have turned away from ceremony of all types. There is often a feeling that civilized people do not need ritual.

Ritual is something for savages, but we are wiser and we 'know' there is no point in leaping about in a bear skin. However, in lives less colourful for want of ritual, unacknowledged rituals often lurk, pulling strings from the corners. In fact, our lives are much more difficult for want of social rituals, that may have been dismissed as stuffy and old fashioned.

For instance, in the nineteenth century, social ritual was complex and exact. On moving into the neighbourhood you left your calling card, then your neighbours left their cards with you. From bows and hat-raising, progress was made to 'taking tea' together, and so one made friends and gained acceptance. Romances were similar. A code of conduct meant that one knew where one was, more or less, and what the next move should be and who should make it. Contrast this with the modern agony. 'Should I phone him? After all, it's Women's Lib, isn't it? And yet, I don't want to appear too keen. But what if he's the shy type? He was staring at me – surely that means he fancies me? But what if he has a girlfriend already? Or perhaps he's short-sighted and couldn't see me properly without his glasses? Oh well, perhaps I should wait for him to make the next move. But what if he thinks I'm being unfriendly? . . .' And so it goes on. There will be few people who do not recognize the scenario. While we may welcome a freer atmosphere, there is no doubt that the absence of social ritual makes for anxiety and red faces.

Social rituals are actually designed for our protection, so that we may communicate without misunderstanding or offence. Animals also adopt ritual behaviour, to designate sexual interest, aggression, acquiescence and other states. Because of this, fights to the death are uncommon in the animal kingdom. Survival of the species has built in some safeguards, so that the weaker can save face and retreat, to fight, or mate another day. Perhaps the most common denominator of all ritual is that it eases passage. Change, which is the only constant in life, is facilitated by ritual, and/or marked by it, such as in the 'ritual' of celebrating birthdays.

The purpose of ritual

Ritual can be heard as the dull and boring, or it can have a ring of magic, secrecy and power. The main purpose of ritual in the ceremonial sense is to effect a change of consciousness in those participating. Ritual gets behind the conscious mind to deeper levels. Ritual is important at times of life's passage, such as birth, coming of age, marriage and death. At these times certain predetermined rites and activities can help a person to enter a new state of being, to celebrate that new state, to enter it wholeheartedly in full and deep appreciation of what it means, and to feel this is understood and supported by others in the community.

The only rite of passage that we come close to 'doing' in a proper, ceremonial fashion in our culture is marriage. This is because the romance of the situation appeals to us and it is a magnificent excuse for a large and expensive party! Even so, much remains unacknowledged in the marriage ceremony, such as the demanding nature of the bond, the radical change in commitment and, today, the very alive possibility of divorce! Gypsy weddings, where blood is mingled and the broomstick jumped, mark the rawer aspect of the union and its sexual and fertile connotations, where the old vows made 'for a year and a day' were rather more realistic in terms of human inconstancy.

Virtually no rituals exist in our culture for young girls reaching the menarche, or boys becoming young men. It is this age group that gives society the most trouble. Adolescent rebellion is accepted, even regarded as a sign of psychological health. However, in more 'primitive' societies it is relatively unknown, as the young take their places with honour, beside their elders. For death, despite funeral arrangements, we have inadequate systems, that do not give room to the bereaved to grieve fully and move on, nor accord to the dying person the means to ease their passage into the next stage of existence. For all these immense changes in life, we are hungry for the right ritual.

Religious ritual

In most religious systems, ritual is used as a means of drawing closer to deity. In Christian denominations, rituals range from highly complex and atmospheric Catholic and High Church services, complete with incense, robes and effigies, to those where ritual is regarded as suspect, even heathen. Churches are bare, services simple and homely, the presupposition being that trappings 'get in the way' and that others 'worship statues'. Each person obviously has the right to choose his or her preferred mode of worship, or nonworship, but those who eschew ritual are missing the point, that it is a means to an end, that it is a celebration and that it is beautiful.

Pagan spiritual paths, such as Wicca/witchcraft, druidry, Northern Tradition, shamanism and similar are experiencing a resurgence in popularity. These ways have many differences in approach, but they are united in the honour they give to Nature and the right they uphold of each person to follow her or his own truth. These systems could be called 'religions'. However, religion has come to mean a set of rules, dogma and beliefs. While paganism has its mythological inspiration, its reverence and one rule, generally held, which is 'Harm none', the pagan way is essentially about what you do and what you are, rather than what you 'believe' as cast in marble. Another distinguishing trait of pagans is their habit of worshipping the Goddess, either in place of or alongside the God, thus Femininity and all that includes and implies (which is broad) is honoured. Pagans are more interested in experiencing the Goddess and God within the natural world, and within themselves, than laying down a code of rules. A recipe for chaos and strife? Pagans say not. They point to the times beyond number in history when domagtic beliefs have been behind destruction and killing, and they feel that their approach has a unity of feeling and intention.

Much pagan ritual centres upon the seasonal cycles of the

sun and the earth, and we shall be looking at these in a later chapter. Cycles of the moon are also honoured. This has the effect of connecting the individual with her or his Source, which is the purpose of all ritual that we may call 'religious' and is an ingredient also in rites of passage.

Ritual and magic

The most exciting meaning of 'ritual' is connected to magic. There is an underlying belief that, if we do or say the right things in the right order, we will get what we want and open the enchanted door. Popular superstitions are connected to the belief that certain actions can bring about certain results by some means other than cause and effect – such as bad luck from walking under a ladder. Often there is some sound symbology underlying this. When we are young we more readily revert to 'magical thinking' – 'everything will be all right as long as I don't step on any of the cracks in the pavement'. As we mature we leave this behind in favour of the rational approach. Indeed, 'magical thinking' is considered by psychotherapists as a sign of mental or emotional instability. However, if you take the view that we are architects of our own reality in a very real sense, magical thinking brings results. Not stepping on the cracks can be a little ritual to convince ourselves that we can indeed structure our lives. However, this is rather negative. It is a way of achieving an illusion of control, when we feel fearful and powerless, and in a sense we relinquish control in such a ritual, for it often turns into 'I *must not* step on the cracks, or something dreadful will happen'. True magical ritual is a set of actions to convey intent, to focus the consciousness and to bring about change.

Magic, as defined by the magician Aleister Crowley, is the art of causing change to occur in conformity with the will. The change first takes place in the mind of the practitioner and extends into the ether, cosmos, call it what you will.

Metaphysicians in ever greater numbers tell us that it is we who create our own reality. Things don't happen to us, they happen because of us, manifesting our conscious and unconscious beliefs and expectations. The only reason that we are able to ignore this, and argue with it is because of the time lag. Things take a while to happen and some take many years. In the higher dimensions, we are told, our visualizations take on immediate reality. Here, although it is a slower process, it is equally real. Scientific thinking, of course, rules this out. Science is the current tyrant, the sanctified dogma, although at the cutting edge, scientists are realizing that mind is present within all matter. One current joke tells how the most advanced and able scientists, when hauling themselves up the last few gruelling yards of the slope of Knowledge, come exhausted to a green and fertile place – and find that theologians and spiritual leaders have already been sitting there for centuries!

Sensible magical workers do not expect scientific laws to disappear, for the apple to rise from the ground and afix itself back to the branch. They work within our reality perception, as it is at present, concentrating for the most part on changes within their own consciousness. One of the most important statements I have ever read concerning magic was written by J. H. Brennan in *Experimental Magic* (see Further Reading). He states that magic works in the direction of belief, not intent. It is what you believe that will materialize, not what you want and, if you don't really believe that something will come into your life, all the spells and rituals in the world are most unlikely to have any effect. However, there is an exception to this and it arises with the unconscious mind. Symbols are powerful things, and despite conscious disbelief, if the inner you, your Younger Self, is convinced, you never know . . .

Spells are a way of 'spelling out' what you want. You can achieve little or nothing in life without knowing what you want, defining it, being exact about it. Spells focus intent. Magical ritual alters consciousness, making change possible. The shift takes place, the call goes out. The results come back, sometimes quickly, sometimes slowly, and often in ways we do not immediately recognize, but come back they do. Magical spells and rituals are the subject of a later chapter.

Meaningless ritual

Here we come to the unacceptable face of ritual, where it is not so much the individual that performs the ritual as the ritual that owns the individual. This happens to most of us at some time and ranges from things we do 'because we have always done them' to the sort of compulsive behaviour we met in Prologue II, that arises from extreme anxiety. All 'meaningless' rituals arise to some extent from anxiety, a fear that things won't be the same, or we won't be 'okay' if we don't carry on as we always have. This sort of ritual is not the same as a tradition, which connects us with the past, giving us a sense of continuity and celebration. If your family have 'always' had a roast meal in Sundays, maybe that has real meaning for you in life, as family bonding, etc. Or maybe not. Perhaps the bonding has turned to bondage and you would all prefer to do something else, especially the person who has to cook the meal! It is up to you to look at such rituals and decide whether they are performing a meaningful function.

Other rituals could be the morning shower, washing the car, arranging shoes neatly before going to bed, and other multitudinous possibilities. Now all these things have a basic usefulness and a sound symbology. Your shower gets you clean and it symbolically cleanses your mind for a fresh start. Washing the car may give you pleasure as you are taking care of a valuable possession and also putting on a good face to the world. Even arranging your shoes may signify order in life and will mean you know where to find them in the morning. It is only when these habits become tyrannous that they need examination. Can't *ever* do without a shower each morning, even when leaving at 4:00 a.m. to catch a plane? Can't *ever* go out on Sunday with a dirty car? Just can't sleep if your shoes are in separate corners of the bedroom? Then something needs looking at.

Using daily activities as rituals is a good idea. In fact, the 'ritual bath' is a recognized magical act and can be used for several purposes or as a fitting precursor to ritual. There is a lot to be said for turning daily activities into rituals – sweep out your bad mood with the duster, wash something troublesome down the drain with your shower. However, if you simply can't bear to do without some ritual activity, if you are chained to it, if it rules your peace of mind, deprives you of choices, or if, in extreme cases, it is the only way you can control your anxiety, it is time to take it by its horns and eject it from your life. Ritual needs to work for you.

Practice

Examining those habits

You can make ritual a positive tool that works for you, expanding your life and giving you direction. This can be an exciting and often beautiful pathway to a new perspective on existence. But, first, it is a good idea to root out the old 'rituals' that aren't working positively for you.

First, examine how you spend your time. You can do this by sitting down and thinking your way through your day, jotting down everything on a piece of paper. Or you can monitor yourself as you go along. Wherever you find yourself involved in some repetitive, compulsive action for no good purpose, take note.

Some people have little or no 'meaningless' rituals in their lives. This is obviously good, but depends somewhat on the reason. Is it due to sensible attitudes, or is it down to laziness, hopelessness, incapacity? At least the performance of ritual means we feel we can have some effect. The point is, could we be more effectual? In addition, could we also be more joyful, spontaneous, creative?

When you have singled out your senseless rituals, if you have any, decide to go about changing them. You may be the sort of person who readily makes changes, it only needed someone to draw your attention to the pointlessness of it and you get rid of it, and so forth. Do what you feel comfortable with. If you are the sort of person who finds it hard to change, think carefully about what you need to change, and introduce these changes piecemeal, slowly but with determination. You may find the first few times really hard, but gain in momentum as you feel a sense of release. Understanding friends and family members (who do *not* have their own agenda in the matter, such as getting you out of the bathroom earlier!) can be enlisted to help, support, remind and encourage. The purpose here is to free you and to empower you, so that you have the time and energy in your life to make ritual work for you.

2

construction
of ritual

And round and round the circle spun
Until the gates swing wide ajar,
That bar the boundaries of earth
From faery realms that shine afar.

The Witch's Ballad, Doreen Valiente

Rituals can be conducted in several ways and many are informal. However, for a consciously directed, purposeful ritual, certain trappings are desirable. These come in a variety of guises, clothing, tools, symbols, effigies, and their basic intent is to change the consciousness of the person performing the ritual, focusing the mind towards the intent specified. However, what most people find along the way is that the goal may become irrelevant, especially if it was essentially frivolous, and the inward change that is wrought tends to become the most important aspect, for by performing rituals we may bypass the conscious Policeman part of the mind, escape the straitjacket of 'rationality' and draw closer to our spiritual source.

Witchcraft

The way we set about ritual will depend to a large extent upon our tradition, training and beliefs. My background is hedge-witch, Wicca and some bits that are no doubt my own. A 'hedge-witch' is a dweller on the thresholds, on the boundaries, in the shadows. Boundary areas, such as hedges, were sacred and mysterious spots to the Celts, on whose traditions much of witchcraft is supposedly based. Hedge-witch also has a delightful ring of one who looks for wild herbs and mushrooms among the hedgerows! Witchcraft is fully discussed in *Witchcraft* in this series. Witchcraft has nothing at all to do with 'devil-worship', for witches do not believe in the devil, and there is nothing about the craft that anyone could reasonably term evil, in fact, very much the reverse.

Witchcraft is 'wise-craft'. Why, then, use the term, some ask, when it is so frightening? Why not call it something else? This begs the whole question of why witches have been persecuted and why the term is 'frightening'. For now, suffice to say that most witches are reluctant to leave behind a word in the name of which so many of their sisters and brothers have died, and to 'sell out' to those who are prejudiced or dogmatic. However, the 'W word' is used sparingly, for there isn't any point raising unnecessary hackles. In addition, 'witch' can be a bit posey. Basically, witches are Nature worshippers, to the majority of whom the Goddess is of immense importance. Witches celebrate the cycles of Nature, in all her guises, inwardly and outwardly, and seek to develop their own personal effectuality, as 'power to' not 'power over'.

The magical tools that I shall be describing are thus principally 'witchy'. However, their symbolism is fairly universal. Of course, you are free to devise symbolic tools of your own, if you wish. It is sometimes said that symbols and implements have no 'real' power, but that their sole power rests in the state of mind that they evoke in the practitioner. Maybe so, maybe not. I think to assume this exclusively is to miss something about the essential nature of magic. However, it matters little. Symbols do their job.

The power of symbols

A symbol is a sign that evokes a chain of meaning and association in the mind, consciously, unconsciously or both. An example of this is the Christian cross that speaks of so many things and so many historical events, but principally it proclaims that Christ died for us, to redeem us. So it means suffering, eternal life and Christian unity. People who are not Christian may feel it emphasizes the 'suffering' aspect too much, and that this has coloured our culture. The cross is powerfully evocative for all of us. The cross with the extended downward stem is a development of the more ancient, equal-armed cross, often enclosed in a circle and called the Celtic Cross. This cross signifies balance and completeness, our earthly state governed by the four cardinal directions, the four elements of Earth, Fire, Air and Water, and others. This has a recognized magical significance and is used by pagans. In addition to general and archetypal significance, symbols also have personal meaning. For instance, the cross might represent to you crashing boredom if you were forced into unhappy hours at Sunday school, or it could mean indescribable spiritual transcendence if you experienced vivid enlightenment in a church.

Another well-known symbol is the pentagram, or five-point star. This is also called the pentacle. Strictly speaking, the pentacle is the disk on which the star is engraved, but the terms are used interchangeably by many people. The pentagram is much associated with witchcraft. Shown with one apex pointing, upwards it means the power of human intent working creatively with the four elements, or it can be also taken to mean the four traditional elements, along with the fifth element, Ether. A pentagram shown with one apex pointing downwards and two upwards, like horns, looks like a goat's face and has been taken to represent evil. However, the goat is the Horned God of Nature and the downward apex is the spark of the divine within the natural world, something that has been forgotten and neglected as people have striven to 'rise above' the world of matter. The pentagram can also be seen as the female body, while the six-point star can be taken as the masculine. The pentacle is usually placed on pagan altars to represent the element of Earth.

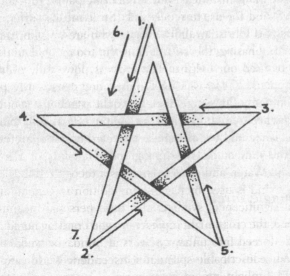

The pentagram is a sign that is often drawn in the air, during rituals, starting with the top point of the apex, passing down and to the right, and so forth (see diagram) in what is called an 'Earth invoking' pentagram, closing by repeating the down-stroke. This is an excellent general symbol to master for ritual work, or anything esoteric, for it has strong protective, evocative qualities. Such symbols really do have a power of their own, as was demonstrated recently to me.

At a talk and demonstration of dowsing, given by the healer and dowser, Colin Pope, the energy field of a glass of water was mapped. Most, if not all things have an 'energy field' which can be detected by dowsing, if one is so programmed and, of course, finding water is the traditional job of the dowser. Colin approached the glass of water with his rod and detected a field about 15 centimetres (6 inches) or so around the rim of the glass. He then invited a member of the audience to bless the water. I was the one who volunteered, and I walked up and inscribed a pentagram in the air, over the glass of water. I have done similar things in rituals time after time, but on this occasion I was stiff and self-conscious. I didn't visualize or concentrate, I just made the symbol and stepped back. Colin again produced his dowsing rod and this time the energy field around the water had extended to 2 metres (6 feet)! 'Powerful symbol, that,' he remarked. He was right. I had not consciously put anything into my 'blessing' apart from the symbol itself. So symbols can be strong things and we can put our trust in them, in rituals. Most, if not all spells have a symbolic content, although this may not be anything grand.

The magic circle

The magic circle is the place where magical endeavour takes place and takes shape. The circle is a 'world between the worlds'. While in circle we are neither in this world nor in Otherworld, but in a kind of halfway house, where our contact with the 'ordinary' world has not been severed, but where our actions are also felt on the astral plane. By virtue of its perfect, symmetrical shape, the circle can touch other dimensions. This circle has a protective function, because when we are doing ritual we may attract forces or beings that could give us problems. However, the circle is also, and perhaps principally, a containment field, where we are raising power, which we do not wish to dissipate until the time is right.

Traditionally, the circle is 9 feet in diameter, marked out by a cord of 4 feet 6 inches. No metrication, please! These are measurements that have a sound basis in megalithic culture. However, circumstances for rituals vary and, if there are to be many people present, one may wish for a larger circle. In my case, the area in which I work is smaller. We all have to work with what is available, and practical. It is usual to place an altar in the north of the circle. (Southern Hemisphere dwellers might like to reverse this. North is chosen because it is the dark side of the sky, where sun and moon do not appear, thus it is the realm of mystery and 'inwardness'.) Symbolic articles are placed on the altar, some of which we shall be encountering, and candles may be placed at each of the quarters, forming a complete temple.

First, let us work with a 'shorthand'. Simply get into the habit of imagining a protective bubble around you, for the magic circle is actually a sphere, in three dimensions. Spend some time doing this regularly, say five minutes a day, until it comes easily. If you can't visualize, use props, such as a circular rug. If other senses are more vivid for you than the visual, employ them. 'Hear' your circle, a humming power-field around you. 'Feel' it tingling. 'Smell' its presence, in a lingering hint of incense. Simply form it about you by holding your arm extended, pointing a finger and drawing it in the air. Tell yourself it is there.

Cleanse the space of your circle, whether it is a small one, close about you, or much larger. Traditionally, the witches' besom is used to sweep the area, but you can just wave your hands and blow, if you wish, imagining all negativity being driven away by your motions. Remember, there is no such thing as 'just' imagination, for imagination is the root of all creativity. To some extent it is true that the more you put into a ritual, the more you will get out of it. Thus, if you put a lot of effort into creating the ambience and power of a full magical circle, what you do is likely to have greater effect. However, a less formal approach can suffice. Some people cleanse their circle after it is formed, some cleanse the space prior to formation. I usually take the latter approach, but I do not think it matters. The circle is 'programmed' to release what you intend to release, so if you cleanse it after you have made it, impurities will go out through its skin, like perspiration through human skin.

The four elements

Western magical traditions identify four basic elements, which have nothing to do with atomic construction, but are rather four States of Being. Probably they are already familiar to you. They are Earth, Fire, Air and Water. Each sign of the zodiac belongs to one or other of these elemental groupings, denoting four basic attitudes, and you may find the element of your sign especially harmonious for you, when performing ritual. Each element is also linked to a direction. Traditions do vary somewhat, but I will give the association adopted by most witches. Readers in the Southern Hemisphere may like to rotate the associations through 180 degrees, so that North corresponds to Fire, because for you the sun is in the north.

Fire is the element of inspiration, initiative, energy, enterprise, passion, get up and go. It is transformative, but so is Water. Fire is about the transformations of the spirit. It is about seeing beyond, following one's beacon, discerning meanings, believing in possibilities. The zodiac signs Aries, Leo and Sagittarius are Fire signs. The Fire spirits are the Salamanders. Fire is associated with the South (in the Northern Hemisphere). The south wind is called Notus. It is also associated with the prime of life, with midday, and with summer.

Earth is the element of practicality, grounding, solid results, security, common sense, Mother Wit, fertility and reality as we know it. Earth requires special honour, as it embodies our physical state (and Gaia has been poorly treated). Earth is about keeping one's feet on the ground, about what works, feels good. The zodiac signs Taurus, Virgo and Capricorn are Earth signs. The Earth spirits are the Gnomes. Earth is associated with the North. The North wind is called Boreas (pronounced '*Borus*'). It is associated with Winter, midnight and old age and death/reincarnation.

Air is the element of thought, intellect, communication, movement, mind and consciousness. Air is about thinking, reflecting, meditating. This element is about staying detached, while in contact, and using one's mind, in whatever way, to take effect. Air can be associated with the purely cerebral, but properly it is not merely that – it is the inventive mind at work in the environment, and thus the home of the Magician. The zodiac signs Gemini, Libra and Aquarius are Air signs. The Air spirits are the Sylphs. Air is linked to youth, to dawn and to spring. Air is associated with the East and the east wind is called Eurius (pronounced '*Yoo-rus*').

Water is the element of feeling, human bonds, emotions of love, pity, caring, empathy, wordless wisdom and intuition of the quieter type (not the Fiery 'flashes'). Water dissolves differences, accepts, soothes, cleanses – and yet remembers. The Water zodiac signs are Cancer, Scorpio and Pisces. The Water spirits are called Undines, and Water is linked to the direction West. The west wind is called Zephyrus. The West is connected to maturity and also old age and sojourn in the Underworld, for the Blessed Isles of the dead were held to be in the West.

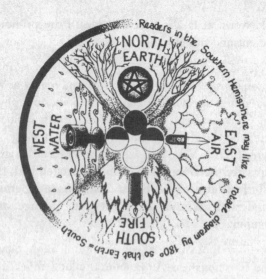

These associations are not cast in marble. They can be set out on a wheel, as shown in the diagram, and incorporated into the magic circle, as we shall see in the step-by-step instructions later. Such circular patterns are also called 'Medicine Wheels' or wheels of power, and there are many options. The Native Americans have different versions of the Wheel, according to tradition, and the Lakota tradition, for instance, equates East with Fire, South with Water, West with Earth and North with Air. The associations I have given are the ones that I, and many others, use. It is up to you, but it is not a bad place to start.

A list of tools

Here is a list of some of the traditional magical tools and their meanings and uses.

Candles These are an obvious magical tool, with many uses, prevalent in all ritual. The simple lighting of a candle is a ritual in itself. Just lighting a candle to a special purpose, such as inner peace, or world peace, can be powerful. Fire is a transformative element and possibly the purest, for Fire cannot be polluted like Earth, Air and Water. In rituals, candles are sacred to the element of Fire.

Candles of different colours can be chosen to signify different purposes. On that subject, let us take the opportunity to look at some colour correspondences – the subject of correspondences will be further addressed later.

Green is associated with money to some extent – however, more on this subject later, when we look at money spells. Green or blue can be healing. Green is also for fertility, creativity and growth, for happiness, peace and love, emotion, instinct and the powers of Nature. Balance and harmony. Connected to the element of Water.

Blue is about harmony, clarity, friendship and compassion. Also loyalty, sincerity and love, justice, wisdom, administration. Connected to the element of Air.

Yellow signifies transformation. At the time of writing yellow seems to be gaining in popularity; I have painted my study a buttery yellow, for yellow is the colour for the mentality, eloquence and divination, seemingly especially appropriate for our changing and inspiring times. Yellow is creative and active. Some people connect it with Earth – I do not share this.

Red is for courage, strength, defence, exorcism, desire, energy, passion and dynamic healing of organs, especially after surgery. It is associated with the element of Fire and with the full moon and the Goddess as Mother.

Orange is for health, enlightenment, communication, success, energy, progress, travel, leadership, intellect and it can also be protective.

Purple, or royal blue, aids meditation, promotes contemplation and psychism and lends depth and majesty. This could be good in spells over legal settlements.

Black candles are the most sombre of all, but definitely not sinister or malevolent. Black is associated with the Crone aspect of the Goddess. This denotes receptivity and serious intent. Also binding and secrecy.

Brown is a protective colour, connected to concentration, grounding and absorption. Obviously the colour brown can be incorporated into rituals. Candles of that colour are rarely seen, but a muddy plum colour can be found. Dark green could be a substitute, or a honey colour. Brown is the colour of the element of Earth.

Different colours of candles and other trappings may be used to mark the various festivals, as we examine elsewhere. Not everyone agrees with the above correspondences and, in any case, these overlap. Whatever your purpose, choose a colour that feels right to you. When in doubt, you can't go wrong with **white**, which is specifically linked to purity, children and expansion.

Wand Yes, magical practitioners really do use wands! Some traditions associate wands with the element of Fire and, so, with inspiration. Some link the wand to Air and to swift and clear thought. I take the former view, for to me wands have sparks at the tip, and I use a wand to conduct and generate energy. Wands can be of fallen wood, or wood that you select – always ask the tree first. A wand can be a simple piece of thick twig, oiled for preservation and suppleness, or it can be much more ornate with a stone or crystal at the tip.

Athame This is pronounced '*athAYmee*'. It is a blunt knife, used for ritual purposes, but never for cutting. We may link this to the element of Air and to the 'cutting edge' of the intellect, although some traditions equate the athame with Fire. You can use the athame to direct concentration; for instance, it can be used to mark out your magic circle.

Pentacle We met this earlier, as the five-point star, usually associated with the element of Earth.

Chalice, cauldron and/or **bowl** Linked obviously to the element of Water, and to the Feminine aspect of creation. Chalices and cauldrons appear often in myth and are deeply magical.

Incense Incense is associated with Air. You can burn stick incense, such as a joss stick, or go to the trouble of burning combustible incense over charcoal. This is far preferable and I think it is best to use a small censer so that the incense can waft about, rather than a thick bowl which will have to remain static. Do be careful where and how you burn incense – don't use an old ashtray which will become very hot. Practise a little with the charcoal first. It may require patience, but it is worth it.

Other extras For any ritual you do, you may like to search within yourself and in a variety of books for symbols and artefacts that are appropriate. Go with what feels right to you and evokes the correct response. I would always choose to have a devotional object for the Goddess and one for the God present, for in this way the forces of Creation are honoured. This could be a picture or pictures, special shaped stones, statues or whatever. You may place flowers in your work area which ideally needs to include an altar as a ritual base, although for simple spells this isn't necessary. Anything seasonal, such as fruit, nuts, foliage, is also a good idea, especially for seasonal workings. If you wish to make sounds, include a bell which has many ritual uses, signifying beginnings and endings and being rung a symbolic number of times. A drum is great for beating out a rhythm, and if you or someone else taking part can play a penny-whistle, then the great god Pan himself will be with you! In addition, you will need to have with you anything special to the spell or ritual that you are intending to perform

– gifts, garlands, wine, food, cords, paper and pen, crystals, or whatever. It's also a good idea to have some notes handy, because all sense can go out of the window once you get into 'drifty' mode.

Clothes Some witches work their rites naked, because they feel that way they can draw closer to their essence, be closer to Nature, more honest, untramelled and leave the energy currents from the human body more free to circulate. Some also say that there is less likelihood of attracting mischievous entities to one's workings if one is naked, as exposed genitals are said to scare off demons! This is probably the original purpose behind the placing of the Sheila-Na-Gig – the Hag with the yawning vulva – on churches, such as the church at Kilpeck, in Hereford, England. No doubt this arises from the ancient belief that the exposed genitals of the Goddess brought life and healing and, by association, human genitals also have this power.

There is no doubt that a special atmosphere and sensation is generated by naked working, and for esoteric rites it can be very powerful. However, there can be drawbacks of a practical nature and nakedness can be distracting and embarrassing, which doesn't help the magical concentration. Obviously for exoteric rites, those that involve friends and family, you can't go naked. It is a good idea to have a ritual robe that you slip on and keep for magical ritual alone. That way the 'vibes' build up more strongly and you will associate the robe with the required state of mind, so it will be like slipping into 'magical consciousness'. It is also a good idea to have a special piece of jewellery that you wear only for ritual. This could be a string of stones such as amber, amethyst, carnelian, or it could be a symbol on a chain.

More about numbers

The Greek philosopher Pythagoras is credited with giving characteristics to numbers, although the ancient Greeks have been found to be plagiarists who often took over older knowledge and made it their own. Pythagoras taught that in addition to expressing quantity, numbers were also expressive of *quality*. For ritual purposes it can be useful to bear in mind the few associations listed below, when deciding how many candles, how many rings of the bell, etc. Of course, you do not have to incorporate numbers into your ritual at all, unless you wish.

One Unity, solitary, unique, contemplative, spontaneous, single-minded, focused, new start, commitment, determination, purity. The Source. The Ego.

Two Objectivity, balance, polarity, pair-bonding, relatedness.

Three Vitality, creativity, potential, enjoyment, union of opposites, the arts, the family (as in Mother, Father, Child).

Four Manifestation, the material state, groundedness, challenge, practicality, the four elements, law, solidity, solidarity, rootedness and balance.

Five Inventiveness, artistry, talent, knowingness, life, creativity, exploration and expansion.

Six Productivity, co-operation, domestication, usefulness, home-making, marriage.

Seven Hidden wisdom, contemplation, psychism, magic, time and space.

Eight Justice, purpose, cause and effect, leadership and organisation, building up or breaking down (as may be appropriate).

Nine Philosophy, inspiration, humour, philanthropy, leadership (of community, in a caring manner), healing.

Ten Completeness, fulfilment, manifestation (ten fingers, ten toes), capability, achievement.

Higher numbers also possess their own, increasingly subtle meanings. **Twelve**, for instance, is the number of completion, of cyclicity, and **thirteen** is one of the numbers of the moon and all 'lunar' or instinctual matters. If you wish to incorporate number symbolism effectively in your rituals you may wish to research further, beginning with other titles in this series (see Further Reading).

Choice of incense

In setting the scene for your ritual, perhaps the most important ingredient is incense, for scent has a hotline to the instinctual, preverbal slots in the brain and will change consciousness deeply and quickly. If you are serious about your rituals I do recommend raw incense, for while some joss sticks are fine, it can be quite difficult to ascertain what has gone into the making of them, when they are given names like 'Taliesin' and 'Aphrodisia'. Of course, if you are familiar with a particular brand, you may feel happy with what the scent evokes for you, and that is fine.

Raw incense can be purchased in many New Age shops and is usually made up into a recipe. Here one runs into the same problem as with joss sticks – you can't be sure what's in the mix and, while that may not matter if you are burning your 'Beltane' incense at Beltane, there is a lot to be said for making your own, simple incenses. Here is a selection of recipes with easy-to-obtain ingredients, some of which will be in your supermarket while others are obtainable at New Age shops or by mail order. If you cannot obtain the dry ingredients you could incorporate the corresponding essential oil; these are easy to come by at natural therapy centres. Some suppliers are listed at the end of this book.

Good general incense Frankincense, myrrh, cinnamon.

Protection Frankincense, myrrh, clove.

Love Rose, sandalwood, apple blossom, willow, broom, lavender.

Purification Pine, juniper, cedar.

Prosperity Frankincense, cinnamon, lemon (or lemon balm), orange peel, mace, copal.

To banish negativity Two parts each of sandalwood, bay, rosemary.

Healing Myrrh, rose petals, orange peel, eucalyptus, cedarwood.

To aid psychism Frankincense, sandalwood, cinnamon, nutmeg, orange peel/oil, clove/clove oil.

Intelligence Four parts benzoin, two parts mace, one part marjoram, one part lavender/lavender oil.

It's worthwhile investing in the more expensive gums like frankincense which is wonderfully majestic, and benzoin which is powerfully mind-clearing. By experimenting you will find blends that suit you.

The right state of mind

I have always believed that acquiring the right state of mind is an important part of any ritual, because it opens the pathways to the ether, so to speak, besides expanding the spirit. Much of any ritual is devoted to changing the state of consciousness of the practitioner anyway. However, spells sometimes work when the practitioner doesn't believe in them, or when little effort is actually put in, such as my 'blessing' of the water. Something strange and mysterious is indeed at work here. However, I do not advocate a careless approach, because these things deserve to be taken seriously, if playfully – 'mirth with reverence'. Nor do I recommend doing a spell in a spirit of experiment, 'just to see'. The universe has a sense of humour and the laugh could be on you. Most likely, nothing will happen, and nothing will be proved.

Getting in the right state of mind is mostly the point of magical ritual. It starts with relaxation, and total relaxation, while a most simple thing, is hard to achieve. If you wish to become proficient at rituals then daily practice of conscious relaxation is a good start and will benefit you generally, into the bargain.

Choose a time of day to practise your relaxation and decide that you will do it *every day*. Five minutes spent daily is better than an hour, once a week. Morning or evening may be best, and devote as much time as you can to it without getting bored and without overstretching your schedule. The most important thing is that you keep it up, for this is a ritual in itself and will be strengthened by habit. I suggest that you start with ten minutes and work up to half an hour, or more, if you wish. Try not to miss a day. If you do, forgive yourself, start again, and tell yourself you won't miss any more. Or, if you must, take one day off a week, then limit yourself to that.

Settle yourself on your bed, for that will suggest relaxation to your unconscious mind. As you become more adept you may wish to move to a chair, so you do not fall asleep. Concentrate on your body, using whatever means most appeal to let go of tension. Some people favour the tensing of each muscle in turn to unbearable intensity, and then relaxing. I think that's a good way to get cramp. Just allow all the tenseness to flow out of you, as if a river of light is passing through you, or you are rocking on the waves of an unseen ocean. If you prefer, you could imagine that all your muscles are powered by little people who now, in response to your command, are downing tools and walking out. Whatever your preferred method, go through your whole body slowly, either from head downwards, or feet upwards, spending special time with the multitude of tiny facial muscles. Check, and check again, gently and lovingly rooting out any pockets of tension and liberating them.

When you feel that you are successful in relaxing you may progress to rhythmic breathing; in a 2/4 sequence, breathe in to a count of four, hold for a count of two, breathe out to a count of four, hold for a count of two. Use your abdominal muscles, not your throat, and do not strain at any time. After a while your mind will associate this rhythm with relaxation and the process will become effortless. This, in itself, is a ritual that can be of great benefit to you, for when you receive a shock, or are in a state of strain, you can turn on your rhythmic breathing and it will calm you down. I have found that this does work in many life situations, if you can separate yourself for a while from the stressor.

Having achieved this relaxed state, you can now progress to visualization, pathworking or shamanic journeying, if you so wish. These are outside the scope of this book. However, I do suggest two things you may concentrate upon while you are in this state of relaxation. One is building an 'astral temple' – a sanctuary made of mind-stuff, where you may retreat inwardly when you relax. This is a safe base on the subtle planes for any other visualizations or inward journeys you may choose to undertake. Build a place that feels right, don't have a hut on an exotic beach just because it is somewhere you would like to go for a holiday. Often if you ask your inner self, while you are in a state of relaxation, to provide an image of a safe and beautiful haven, one will spontaneously arise for you and might not be as you imagine. Go into your astral temple each time you are in a relaxed state. This will reinforce and strengthen your temple.

Alternatively, an obvious use of your relaxed and open state is the simple visualization of your wishes. If you have a purpose in life such as a job, relationship, travel, then imagine that this is now real. Imagine in delightful detail how it is to receive the letter, get the keys, step off the plane, be in a loving relationship. (Steer clear of erotic imaginings, because you will get distracted!) Affirm to yourself that this is real in your life, not 'going to come' but actually manifesting. Doing this regularly is a powerful tool for progress. If you do these visualizations, don't forget to ground yourself before resuming daily life. This is explained in the step-by-step ritual description.

For the purposes of ritual, this relaxation is of great benefit for it breaks down some of the barriers that we erect against the vast ocean of spiritual power that is available. Having learnt to relax, you may choose to adopt this process before embarking on ritual. Or having perfected the association between breathing and relaxing, you can use it as a short cut, to unwind you, and get you closer to the required state.

Having relaxed, 'ritual' consciousness is well within your grasp, for it is more or less similar to that 'floaty' state we all go through twice a day, as we fall asleep and as we wake up. Attaining this drifty state paradoxically makes you more aware of subtle reality.

Another aspect to state of mind is whether or not you 'feel good' about the whole process. If you do not, I would strongly recommend that you leave it well alone. Remember, magic works in the direction of belief, not intent. If you really do not believe that you can possibly get that job, don't do any spells for it. Choose, perhaps, a general spell for luck and prosperity that you can do with conviction, or just don't do anything and get a good night's sleep, instead. Of course, a negative state of mind may be something you need to address in yourself, but that will need to be done in a general manner, not forced on an issue, for in a battle between the will and the imagination, imagination always wins. Perhaps this particular job is not for you, anyway. Only *you* can distinguish between negative thinking and true intuition.

Correspondences

Correspondences are magical 'links' on the 'like attracts like' principle. We have encountered a few in this chapter, for instance red-energy-Fire-salamanders-south. Thus, if we wanted to compose a ritual to acquire greater energy we are well on our way, using candles of bright red, arranged in the south, using our wand to encourage the Fiery salamanders to crackle into our circle and to energize us! Correspondence tables need to be used with caution, I believe, for rigidity denies spontaneity and, in any case, sometimes it can be difficult for the mind to analyse all the disparate elements, while the intuition centres in on what is essential, straight away. As with most things, a combination of approaches works best and we have to use our rational minds to distinguish the correct path, while giving intuition space to sing out loud and clear. Here is a short table of some useful correspondences, to use for reference. I have grouped these alongside their planetary 'rulers' because this feels best – starting at the top and working down! Also, as you become more experienced, thinking further about things you want to gather for ritual, you will find that reference works usually list plants, precious stones and minerals according to their planetary rulers.

Sun Health, protection, vitality, energy, legal matters, enlightenment, success, fulfilment, creativity, willpower. Orange or gold (some equate orange with Mercury; I do not). The sign of Leo. Lions, cats. Amber, carnelian, diamond, tiger's eye, sunstone. Bay, sunflower, cinnamon, benzoin, frankincense, juniper, copal. All deities connected with the sun – Lugh, Grainne, Apollo. Tarot card The Sun. Sunday.

Moon Home, fertility, family, nurture, rhythm, instinct, natural reaction, healing, gardening, dreams, spirituality, love. White and silver (black could be for waning/dark moon, red sometimes for full moon). The sign of Cancer. Fish, dolphins, snake, dog, bear. Aquamarine, chalcedony, quartz, moonstone, mother-of-pearl. Lemon, lemon balm, myrrh, eucalyptus, mallow. All deities connected with the moon – Diana, Artemis, Hecate, Selene (goddesses may differ according to moon phase, and moon gods are somewhat thin on the ground, although in many cultures the moon was originally masculine; Egyptian Thoth is a moon-god). Tarot card The High Priestess. Monday.

Mercury Intelligence, thought, reflection, communication, travel, study, eloquence, divination, wisdom, commerce. Yellow (see note under 'sun'). The signs Gemini and Virgo. Monkeys, swallows (and any small, swift bird). Agate, aventurine, mottled jasper. Lavender, fennel, parsley, mace. Gods and goddesses connected with commerce, travel, creative thought – Mercury/Hermes, Bride. Tarot card The Magician. Wednesday.

Venus Love, harmony, beauty, youth, joy, happiness, reconciliation, pleasure, friendship, compassion, meditation. Blue, pink/rose, also green. The signs Taurus and Libra. Doves, swans. Emerald, lapislazuli, turquoise. Thyme, rose, ylang-ylang, mint (sometimes given to Mercury), feverfew, cowslip, primrose and many flowers with five petals. All gods and goddesses of beauty and love – Aphrodite, Adonis, Oshun, Freya, Edain. Tarot card The Empress. Friday.

Mars Courage, energy, assertion, healing (after surgery), desire, passion, sexuality, strength, defence, exorcism. Red. The signs Aries and Scorpio. Rams, scorpions, horses. Bloodstone, flint, red jasper, garnet, ruby. Wormwood, ginger, basil, peppermint, cumin. Gods and goddesses of war – Thor, Ares, Amazons, Valkyries, Morrigan, Badb. Tarot card The Tower. Thursday.

Jupiter Prosperity, good fortune, luck, justice, legal settlements, spiritual and religious matters, philosophy, long-distance travel, psychism, meditation, expansion, positive attitude. Purple. The signs Pisces and Sagittarius. Centaur, horse, eagle. Amethyst, lepidolite. Sage, clove. Goddesses and gods of majesty, justice and luck – Juno, Zeus, Ishtar, Felicitas, Kuan-Yin (N.B. Kuan-Yin is a powerful goddess of many meanings). Tarot card Wheel of Fortune. Tuesday.

Saturn Binding, grounding, protecting, centring, purifying, nurturing, fertilizing, actualizing, ending, preserving, certain kinds of luck, solidity, restriction. Black, grey, dark brown, dark green and sometimes dark blue. The signs Capricorn and Aquarius. Goats and horned animals. Apache tear, jet, onyx, obsidian. Comfrey, patchouli, cypress. Goddesses and gods of necessity, fate, cosmic order, but also of harvest – Cernunnos, Maat, Nokomis. Tarot card The World. Saturday.

The outer 'extra-Saturnian planets, Uranus, Neptune and Pluto are here omitted because they have been comparatively recently discovered and their associations are somewhat debatable. However, some practitioners are researching them.

N.B. While the Greek pantheon is well defined, others are more diffuse. The study of goddesses and gods is a subject in itself and some of the above associations are subjective.

Ethics

What are the ethics of ritual? Simply this: Harm none – but don't be neurotic. Do not try to take something that belongs to someone else – money, job, lover. Do have the courage to become and be yourself, to succeed, enjoy, revel, celebrate. The universe is boundless and it isn't true that by having what we want we deprive someone else. By the act of living we destroy, of course. To satisfy our hunger, animal or plant life dies. Each time we take a walk, small creatures and plants are crushed beneath our feet. We can't help that. As long as we do no intentional harm and have a true reverence for life and care for others, I do not believe we can go wrong.

As for curses, please do not make them, ever, however bad you feel, however you have been treated. I do not preach to those who have been raped, or whose children have been harmed, for *in extremis* much can be forgiven, and I would prefer to leave that complex subject to one side. But on a cerebral, detached level I hold to the rule that one should never intentionally harm another by magic. They will 'get theirs' don't worry. As for binding and restricting, that is another matter and there are certainly cases for binding spells on paedophiles, rapists, murderers – and many such would be glad of it. However, a decision to do a binding spell on another individual is something I feel should be arrived at by discussion in a group of like-minded, understanding and experienced practitioners of magic. It is an immense responsibility, and outside our scope here.

Practice

As a preparation for rituals you may like to begin collecting your own tools, incense, candles and such like. Search in nature, not just in shops, for your athame may be a piece of flint and you can use seashells, stones and feathers in your rituals. Think also about symbols and what they convey to you. Start your own notebook of thoughts and associations. Practise your relaxation.

getting
down to it

Don't agonize. Organize.
Anonymous

This is a practical chapter, in which you will find all the steps to compose your ritual listed in order. Obviously for informal little spells, or for exoteric rituals, much will be irrelevant, but this chapter is intended as a checklist. Chapter 2 contains information and explanation regarding meanings, tools, etc. to which you will need to refer. Here are the steps.

1   **Identify your goal.** This can be important and not as obvious as it seems. For instance, you may wish to do a spell for money, when there is something specific that you want to buy with that money, and the spell/ritual should be performed

with that end in mind, not for hard cash. It is best to allow yourself at least one night, to dream about your purpose and, if you do not literally dream, you will probably wake up thinking more clearly about the business. Keep a notepad and pencil by your bed to record first thoughts. If this is to be a big ritual, allow yourself more time to reflect.

2   **Plan your ritual**. At this point in the proceedings you are devising and planning all the elements. Some people are good at this and find they can think up quite complex rituals, quite easily, while others find this more difficult and tend to stick with similar methods, time after time, and use traditional spells. It may be that those who are more inventive at the planning stage sometimes don't find the abstract parts come so easily, so don't be hard on yourself if you can't think up much. Stick with basics and with correspondences that feel good. Write down the things that you will need and the methods you will use.

3   **Pick your time**. From a purely practical point of view, you do not want to be interrupted during your ritual, so choose a time when pets and children are attended to by someone else, leave your 'phone off the hook, etc. Night-time is traditionally the favourite time for magical workings, as it is the time when the unconscious reigns supreme (and night 'feels right'). Of great importance is *moon phase*. Spells that relate to increase are best done with a waxing moon, those relating to decrease, banishing, etc. are traditionally done when the moon is waning. Full moon is a highly charged, magical time for workings of all sorts, and when the full moon rides high, all things may be possible! Avoid dark of the moon unless you are quite sure what you are about, for at the time of transition from old, waning moon to new waxing moon, the sun and moon are actually 'in conjunction' which means close together in the sky, and in

the same astrological sign, creating a rather specific and potentially unbalanced atmosphere.

4   **Assemble your tools**. At the very least these will be candles and the requirements for your spell. Personally, I think that for any substantial ritual it is bad manners not to honour each of the elements, and the Great Mother. Here, then, is my list of basic requirements:

- **Candles**: two for the altar, one for the South (I don't place candles at each of the four quarters, because space is limited and I have very long hair . . .). Any extra candles for the specific working.
- **Candle-holders and matches**: easily forgotten.
- **Altar**: placed in the North of the circle (or South, for readers in the Southern Hemisphere). This could be just a cardboard box covered with a suitable cloth.
- **Chalice**: simply to honour the Water element, sometimes to hold wine or fruit juice, for consecration in the ritual, placed on that altar.
- **Censer and incense**: in honour of Air and for the ambience. I usually place this in the East.
- **Athame**: also for the element of Air, placed on the altar.
- **Wand**: for the element of Fire, placed on the altar.
- **Pentacle**: for the element of Earth, placed on the altar.
- **Salt**: this is usually on the altar, having been used to purify the circle. It represents Earth and is linked to Aphrodite.
- **Cauldron**: I like to have this with me and place it in the West as it is associated with Water. Water can be placed in it, but the cauldron is useful for rituals, so a **bowl** containing water can be put in the West, leaving the cauldron free. The cauldron is often placed at the centre of the circle. You may wish also to have a bowl of water on your altar. Salt and water are sprinkled to consecrate the circle.

- **Stones**: it is a good idea to have a stone on the altar, to honour Earth (I don't mean crystals, which may indeed form part of your ritual, I mean a plain old stone).
- **Devotional objects**: I have special objects which, for me, represent the Great Mother and the Horned God, which I always place on my altar. Statues, pictures or whatever may be your choice. I would strongly recommend having something of this nature when you do rituals, according to your belief. This connects us to our Source and to the Divine within us and Nature, to something greater than the personal ego.
- **Besom**: the good old-fashioned broom, to sweep out the ritual space.
- **Notebook and pen:** It is a good idea to have this handy. Witches usually keep notes in their 'Book of Shadows'.
- **Seasonal offerings:** if your working is connected to the seasons, have this represented by flowers, fruits, leaves, etc.
- **Specifics for the spell/working:** any special items needed for the spell or ritual that is to be undertaken.

Check you have everything. You don't want to be scuttling about looking for bits after you have started.

5 **Prepare yourself.** For an important ritual a cleansing bath beforehand is an excellent idea, perhaps containing essential oil of lavender, or salt. Put on your robe and/or jewellery, if you are wearing these. Relax and meditate a little. If you have followed the steps as I have listed them, all your equipment will be ready, and you can begin to 'let go' in the knowledge all is properly prepared.

6 **Create and cleanse your sacred space.** Now you are ready to get down to business, so form your circle with your athame, if you have one, or use a finger-tip to define your

circle. Cleanse it, using a besom, or simply by waving your hands and banishing all that is polluted and negative from your area. Visualize all such as grey clouds that are blown from your circle. Affirm that your circle is in place and clear. Feel its presence. This is an important step. If you need to leave your circle after you have formed it, open a 'doorway' with your athame or hand and close it again after you. When you come back, open and close in the same way. Sprinkle salt and water, saying 'Be blessed by salt. Be blessed by water'.

7 **Invoke the elements.** Ask each of the elements to be present, in turn, preferably starting with Earth, in the North (in the Northern Hemisphere). Ritual words for this are given in *Witchcraft* in this series. Alternatively, you can simply say 'Please be with me, Powers of Earth'. Visualize as strongly as you can all the attributes of Earth, as detailed in Chapter 2, being present at that point of your circle, in the presence of the elemental spirits. Think of caves, soil, standing stones. Turn deosil to the East (deosil means 'in the direction of the sun' which is clockwise in the Northern Hemisphere, anticlockwise in the Southern Hemisphere). Ask the Powers of Air to be with you, imagining their characteristics. Think of breezes, mountain-tops, tree-tops swaying in the wind, birds flying. Then turn to the South, asking the Powers of Fire to be present. Think of flames, bright sunshine, fireworks. Turn to the West, inviting the Powers of Water, imagine waterfalls, surging tides, deep, still pools. Welcome each of the elements and thank them for being there. (If you live in the Southern Hemisphere you may wish to start in the South, here invoking Earth, turning anticlockwise to the East, etc.) Your circle and its guardians are now in place. Stand in the centre for a moment or two and feel your centredness.

8 **Blessing.** Turn to your altar and ask your own Goddesses and Gods to be with you, to bless your endeavours. The particular aspect or personification of deities may depend on the type of working. For instance, if this is a love spell it would be natural to especially ask for the blessing of Venus/Aphrodite.

9 **The working.** Now you can proceed with your particular spell or ritual. *Clearly state to yourself the intention of your working*, as you have earlier clarified it to yourself. Imagine it. Concentrate on it. Will it. Perform the spell/ritual. During this you will raise power, either intentionally by dancing, chanting, gesture, or simply by putting your energy into willing the matter to be. Raising power may also be a part of the spell, such as tying knots in a cord, weaving or similar. These are all ways of raising the voltage, enforcing intent and concentration and incorporating symbolism. Concentrate here, but don't screw up your face and eyes with the effort for that will introduce tension, which is unproductive. An element of play is often best. Direct and release the spell, saying 'may it be so' or similar.

10 **Let go.** I am including this as a separate stage, as you must let go of the energies of the spell. Often in all the effort this can be forgotten, almost as if we have to keep going, keep visualizing, keep trying, and the longer the better, never feeling we have quite 'got there'. Not so. If it's complete, let it wing on its way, do its job. Breathe out and consciously release the matter. Otherwise all you'll get is a headache.

11 **Communion.** At this point it is, I feel, important to commune with the Powers of Life, the Goddess and God, however you visualize them. Witches may do this by conse-crating wine, or some such, and drinking it in honour and

celebration (and very pleasant it is, too!). At all events, thank your deities for being present. Contemplate for a while if you wish. You may strongly feel the presence of other beings.

12 **Farewell**. More than one ritual can be conducted at once and, while you have your circle in place, you may like to conduct several rituals. It is always good, I think, to do three: one for yourself, one for a friend and one for the community/world. If this is a seasonal working, the latter could form part of it, such as consecrating some bread at Lammas and breaking it into crumbs outside, after the ritual, as an antidote to famine in the world. When you have completed your rituals and your communion, which may take as long as you wish, thank the Goddess and God for being present, and say 'Farewell'. Do the same in turn for the four elements, thanks and farewell, usually in the same order as you invoked them. Consciously allow your circle to fade.

13 **Grounding**. This is another important step which may be omitted by someone who is starting out on the process of rituals. You can become quite 'spaced out' doing rituals, and while dispersing your circle will do something to bring you back, it is not always enough. So consciously ground yourself by affirming that you are back in everyday reality, eating and drinking, touching your palms to the floor, patting your body all over, or stamping. Or do them all. Now you are back with the world we call 'real' and your workings are over, for the present.

One final point: don't forget that you must also take concrete action. All the spells in the world won't get you a job unless you apply for one.

Practice

An example spell

This is a spell for a new home.

Home and family are under the domain of the moon, therefore choose your correspondences from the list in Chapter 2, under 'moon'. However, it is also about beauty, happiness, fulfilment, and so Venus is relevant. Furthermore, it is about being earthed, having a base, being secure; these bring in the Earth element, and possibly Saturn, as a grounding influence. The Water element is also involved, as it is connected to the emotions and, therefore, to the family and its members.

- **Candles** Because of the above, use green candles, or white.
- **Incense** This could involve moon herbs, such as lemon balm. I would avoid myrrh, because its connotations can be serious. Sandalwood, lemon balm and rose petals with a little frankincense would be a good choice. In *Incense, Oils and Brews* (see Further Reading) Scott Cunningham suggests two parts frankincense, one part sandalwood and a few drops each of eucalyptus, camphor and jasmine oils for rituals involving the home and dreams, but as jasmine is expensive you could substitute ylang-ylang.
- **On the altar** Place a picture of the type of house you would like, even something that represents all the comforts of home, such as a teapot; crescent moon shape, white flowers such as daisies, possibly pearls or quartz crystals.
- **Deities** Goddesses to bear in mind are Roman Hestia, or any aspect of the Great Mother. Brigid/Bride is good

for the 'home fires' and her symbol is a fire-wheel or off-centre cross. This would add verve to your ritual, placed on your altar, and the creativity of Bride would be a great asset. Any goddess statue or picture would be good.

- **For the spell** All you will need for the spell are some stones and a green cloth. However, you should take time gathering the stones. Go for a walk, thinking about your new home and the number of rooms you will need. Be realistic about the number of rooms that will meet the requirements of you and your family, if you have one. If you need two or even three bathrooms, specify this. Naturally have common sense. What you get will need to be within your budget. Gather a stone for each of the rooms. You may like to gather stones of different sizes, according to the dimensions of the room. If you wish to be less specific about numbers, don't gather for rooms but for attributes, such as comfort, south-facing, close to shops. Or just gather one for each of the Elements. If possible, gather from the area where you wish to move.

When you have constructed your circle, ask for the goddess of your choice to be with you. Place your stones in the centre of your circle, or put them in your cauldron. Touch each stone in turn with your wand, visualizing your power and intent entering the stone. Name the stone for its characteristic. You may dance around the cauldron, or stones if you wish, directing the power so raised into the pile of stones.

Now the stones are consecrated and your dream is a reality. Affirm that your home is coming to you, for you have earthed your wishes, built your dream.

Wrap the stones in a green cloth and set them to one side. Place them where you keep your magical tools, or whatever seems appropriate. Finish your ritual in the usual way.

When you get your new home, bury the stones in the garden, or place them around the house/flat, if there is no garden. If you have dedicated them to the Elements, then choose the appropriate corner of the garden to dispose of them.

Don't forget this last step. Your workings have been a part of what has come to pass and these stones are special. Until they are 'planted' you probably won't feel settled in your new home. Mail may go astray, there may be problems with money, choosing decor, finding the things you have packed, making friends — in short, all the things that make you feel grounded and at home. Cleanse the green cloth by passing through incense (and probably a washing machine!). Use it again, if you wish.

4

spellwork

> By all the powers of land and sea,
> By all the might of moon and sun,
> As I do will, so mote it be,
> Chant the spell and be it done.
>
> *The Wytches' Rune*, Doreen Valiente

A general word about spells

Spells are usually playful things and there is no harm having a sense of fun. Fun and play are the currencies of what the writer Starhawk calls 'Younger Self' – our simple, instinctual side with which we are most fully in tune when we are children. However, although 'younger' this aspect of the self is also full of ancient wisdom.

Having said this, there is also a serious aspect to spells and, while we can have a giggle, we should never be flippant or careless. It is written 'Be careful what you desire, for you shall get it'. If you want something badly enough, for long enough, with enough concentration and conviction, the chances are that you will indeed get it, spells or not. If you look back over your life you may see this in action. Ask yourself, how many times have you achieved your desire and found it wasn't what you expected? Sometimes it may have been the devil's own job to get this once-desirable thing out of your life, having willed it in place! So a word to the wise; always ask yourself why you want what you want. Is it a real need, or something you have fixated upon when what you need may be something else? A mundane example might be a desire for an expensive leather coat that turns out not to be warm, or nice to wear, after you've had it for a month or two, and what you needed was something equally stylish but more snuggly. A leather coat is one thing, a relationship is quite another . . . Is what you want a true expression of you, or something that you have been conditioned to want? For instance, do you really want that brand new house, or is it something your mother always wanted when you were little and you'd really feel at home in a country cottage? Selling a house is easier than changing your career path in mid-life. These are just a few examples.

Bear in mind also that the Younger Self, unconscious mind, or whatever, is literal, so always word spells clearly and exactly, as if to a child. For instance, if you badly need loads of new clothes and can't afford them, don't do a spell for a new wardrobe or you may get exactly that – a new wardrobe, in best veneered chipboard.

Children and spells

People are sometimes worried about involving children in

magic. However, most children are natural witches and magicians, because they are utterly focused upon want they want ('Give it to *me*'), have wonderful imagination and can usually concentrate sharply, although for only short periods. Besides this, they are free from so many of the preconceptions and doubts that cluster around us as adults.

As an example of how we 'learn not to believe', the story of the landing in South America of the explorer Magellan illustrates the point. The natives welcomed the Europeans as they disembarked from their boats, but they were totally unable to see the larger ships that had brought them, for to them so immense an ocean-going vessel was simply an impossibility. So all that they could see was the sea, stretching unbroken to the horizon! It is worthwhile absorbing this anecdote and realizing to how great an extent we structure our own reality, and that it is subjective, not objective. Don't be tempted to put this down to the limited intelligence of primitive natives, for it has nothing to do with intelligence and everything to do with conditioning and human attitude.

Needless to say, young children should never be exposed to complex rituals that they do not understand and that could frighten them, or be exploited in any way by adults. Nor is it suitable to initiate them into a spiritual pathway, such as witchcraft, until they are old enough to understand and make choices. However, never underestimate or patronize the magical abilities of young people. My best, most successful spells were done when I was too young to know what I was doing. Children can be useful. Many's the time, on my way into town, I've said to my sons 'We're getting a parking space, where we need one. Visualize it, We need it. We're getting it.' And we do.

Holding on/letting go

Some esotericists advise that we should saturate our lives with the desire for what we want, that we should visualize it, believe it, expect it, tell ourselves it is on its way for every waking moment it occurs to us. Some advise the opposite – do the spell and forget it. This isn't the same as letting go of the spell energy, which you must do. It is about general attitude.

Personally I am mainly in favour of the 'letting go' approach. Do the spell and rest in happy expectation, but get on with life. It isn't that either approach is 'wrong' but that the holding of an idea in your mind usually leads to obsession and frustration because it is hard to maintain a positive attitude. If you start to have doubts it will not do your purpose any good. Of course, if you want something very much it is also hard not to think about it! The best approach is to say, each time the thought comes into your head 'Yes, I want that. It is coming' and consciously blow it into the ether, while you get on with what is possible. My advice is to put all you have into the spells you do and meanwhile enjoy other things.

Occasionally there are things we want that are not 'meant to be'. This isn't intended as an easy way out, or cold comfort to anyone who doesn't achieve something they very much wanted, but it is a hint to 'go with the flow'. As you become used to doing spells, you will find that the 'tuning in and turning on' necessary for magical workings puts you in touch with universal reality, and you get a feeling for what you should work for and what is best left. If you get the strong feeling that something is not intended, leave it alone or you could make matters worse. Alternatively, doing a spell may make you feel more sure.

Sample spells

After studying Chapters 2 and 3, you are now in a position to construct your own spells. However, it is much more reassuring to be given some suggestions. Here is a selection of spells that you might like to try. Some you may prefer to do with full ritual, some don't need it. However, it is always important to imagine your protective circle around you whenever you are getting up concentration and power. Don't forget to disperse it afterwards and ground yourself.

Love spells

Perhaps the most important thing to all of us is to have someone special of our own to love. Ethics and approach are important in love spells, for it is not a good idea to try to 'get' someone specific, however desirable they seem, however perfectly matched to our requirements. This is because, in so doing, we are seeking to influence someone else's actions and interfere with their path. Sex and human nature being what it is, sexy spells often do work, but if a relationship isn't 'meant to be' then trouble generally results for both parties. So if you are going to do love magic, I would strongly suggest that you aim to attract love into your life in a general way, not someone specific. There is no harm in imagining exactly the kind of person you would like, but that is different from directing your efforts towards a real human being. As for trying to pinch someone else's lover – that really is asking for trouble. Look elsewhere.

Magic can be used to improve an existing relationship. If you do this for a couple, make sure they both want this. Doing magic for others is a big responsibility and generally it is best to work for happiness and peace, in a general way, for friends, rather than respond to their avid desires. As for your own existing relationships, you can work to bring more love in, if you wish. If you have doubts about your lover's wishes, work for clarity first. Of course, you could ask your lover if he or she still loves you and wants the relationship. Hopefully they will respond candidly. In this way your lover takes a fair share of the responsibility.

Simple love spells

- Apples are sacred to the Goddess because of the five-point star shape that appears at the centre when the apple is cut, crossways. They are also an underworld fruit, special to the festival of Samhain/Hallowe'en, and we all know how love connects us to our own personal 'underworld'! Cut an apple in half, crossways, and give half to your lover to eat, eating one half yourself. This ensures an undying love and eternal connection. Sharing any fruit partakes of this symbolism. If you don't have a lover but wish to attract one, you could make an apple part of your ritual, consecrating one to the love-goddess in full ritual, cutting it in half, eating one half and burying the other, feeding it to the birds, or floating it downstream. Don't forget to affirm strongly the type of person you want to attract so you do not throw yourself open to all manner of advances. At the least, you may find an apple tree growing from the buried core!

- Carry rose petals or rose quartz crystals, for both of these attract love. Preferably consecrate them in a ritual first.

- It may be cheating to use Feng Shui, as this is an Eastern tradition and here we are primarily concerned with Western ways. However, the Chinese system of Feng Shui (which means wind, water) is extremely popular and effective. It is concerned with the meanings and sacredness of the space we inhabit. This is a complex and delicate art, but there is no harm in cautiously using some of the basics, to effect a specific result. A Feng Shui consultant told me that it is a big mistake to obtain a book on Feng Shui and to go madly reorganizing your home on the basis of it when your life is pretty tidy, anyway. However, for a specific task, you can make a small change and see if it works. Feng Shui is based on the arrangement of the environment and the relationship area of the home is the far right-hand corner. Take your bearings from your front door, whether or not it enters the house from the side, or you have a flat that you enter from a hall or the back of the house. This is still your 'front' door. Where is the far right-hand corner? This is the love and marriage section. If this area has been cut into by irregularities of the building, draw energies back into it by using a crystal at the window. You may merely place a piece of rose quartz in the relationship area, or perhaps a pair of soft toys, or a statue of an embracing couple. There are some lovely candles obtainable that are shaped like a pair of entwined lovers. Here you could choose according to your wish – a red candle for passionate love, blue or purple for soul-mates, etc. I have found such things to work, especially in respect of the money corner, which we shall discuss in the next section. Unless you are prepared to hire a qualified Feng Shui practitioner to comment on your area, you need to keep the changes small and wait a couple of months to see if they take effect before doing anything else. Of course, if your 'love corner' is home to a pile of old magazines, half-eaten packets of biscuits, torn envelopes and a dirty ashtray, I would suggest tidying it up first!

- Simplest spell of all, adopted by a friend of mine: add 'lover' to your shopping list!
- To ensure the continuance of love, break in half a bay twig and each one of the couple keep half. Or feed each other chestnuts.
- Brazil nuts, carried, are a love talisman. Women can also carry ivy. For men, it is best to carry holly.
- To choose between several admirers, take a green rose leaf for each, name them and note which shrivels last. This is the most enduring love. (However, if you are this unsure, perhaps you need to do some spells to make you more decisive!)
- To find love, tie a hair or two taken from your head to a blossoming cherry tree. (The Latin name for this tree is *Prunus avium*. As it is a beautiful tree, why not plant one in your front garden, anyway?)

• If you fear that someone has put a love spell on you, eat pistachio nuts.

A love ritual

From Chapter 3 you should be able to compose a love ritual, but here are some suggestions.

Choose a Friday, when the moon is waxing, or preferably full. Place roses on your altar – choose red for passionate love, pink for affection. Place Venus herbs there, also, if you wish, such as thyme. Have candles of rose pink. Enjoy a long bath first and annoint yourself with rosewater, or ylang-ylang oil. Call on Aphrodite to help you. After you have invoked the elements, ask for the special help of the salamanders, or Fire spirits, to bring you passion, the Water spirits, the undines, to bring emotional fulfilment, the Earth spirits, or gnomes, to endow you with earthy sensuality and knowledge of the senses, and the Air spirits, or sylphs, to bring you communication. In my view all are operative, but you might like especially to focus on one aspect. Then you may proceed to a specific ritual, which may be about empowering a special crystal to wear, or similar. While in your circle, clearly visualize the love you want. Perhaps write down all the attributes of the lover and burn the paper in the flame of a candle, placed in your cauldron. Touch each part of your body, caressing it and loving it, imagining that a lover will soon be doing this. Affirm that the love you want is now entering your life. Don't forget to let the energies go and close down firmly, because this is the sort of spell that can linger, sapping your energies by unfulfilled desire.

Money spells

Second only to love, money is the next thing most of us want. There is so much guilt and prohibition around money that it is hard to get our ideas on the matter straight, and some sources say that one shouldn't do money spells, that they are selfish, etc., continuing the 'money is the root of all evil' tradition. I do not believe this. It is fine to ask for goodies for yourself as long as you do not seek to deprive anyone else. There is plenty in the universe to go round. Try to let go of a poverty mentality. Remember, money is about flow, not stasis, so part with money gladly, where appropriate. Give also to charity where you can and trust that the Great Mother will provide. She will.

However, there are some problematic issues around the subject of money. One is that when we do money spells we are often bedevilled by unconscious guilt, more so than with love spells, and at a deep level we may feel we shouldn't be doing such a spell. This needs to be sorted out in your mind. Remember, magic works in the direction of belief, not intention. If you cannot find an approach that makes you happy, best to leave the subject alone or ask someone else to do a money spell for you if your need is really dire.

Secondly, money is actually an odd thing. We may think of it as gold, greenbacks, or whatever, but it is, in fact, energy. Money is about power to do what you want, energy to direct into various quarters. By itself, it is useless. At a recent talk given by the magical expert Lionel Snell, the essence of money was addressed. Those who are 'in the know' realize that money isn't about 'filthy lucre' and spells that involve the element of Earth and Venus (yes, she can give money too) may be a mistake, because money is Air and so spells for money should be focused on that element. This wisdom apparently derived from a magical worker who was fabulously rich, planning the purchase of his own helicopter, at whose feet international financiers came to sit in adoration! It certainly makes sense that money is Air, for what is it now but figures on a screen, coming and going? Who has their money buried in their garden, or concealed in a tin in the loft? Money is all theory.

Thirdly, often when we do spells for money, it isn't the money we want at all, but something specific it will buy. Sometimes these spells don't work because they have been incorrectly targeted. Sometimes they do and we are fortunate, but we don't realize that it was our money spell all along. This has happened to me, where I have been lucky to be given things and realized that I didn't need the money after all. If this happens to you, don't forget to say 'Thanks' and perhaps to make a little offering to some charity or cause, either of money or time – or spellwork. If you decide you need to do a spell for money, ask what you really want. Is it money to buy you freedom? Well then, why not do your spell for freedom? Or a bigger house? A spell for a new home appeared in Chapter 3.

I do not pretend to have incorporated these concepts totally into my approach. However, witch friends agree with me that money spells are dubious and there are several reasons, apparent in the above. Obviously, if you feel guilty in any way, this will distort things. Cautionary tales abound. One occultist 'stormed heaven' (or was it the other place?) for a specific sum which she badly needed to pay a bill. Afterwards she went out shopping and fell over in a department store, breaking her leg. The money she was awarded in compensation amounted to the exact figure she needed! A friend of mine, driving to work each day in a car that threatened to fall apart each time he went over a bump, repeated over and over 'I *must* have a car that will get me to work. I *must* have a car . . .' This was an impromptu spell. Then his father died and he inherited a nearly-new car. Not a money spell at all, of course, but a result that guaranteed guilt, as money spells sometimes seem to entail. 'I spelt out what I wanted, and look what happened,' he said, sadly. 'Be thankful,' I replied. 'You didn't make your Dad ill, and if you hadn't done your "spell" the car might have gone to your wealthy sister!' This is an illustration of how material things can make us feel bad. The first step in doing money spells is to ensure that you won't feel 'bad' if you are affluent!

Simple money spells

- Carrying the buds or leaves of poplar is said to attract money. Actually, as trees are related to the Air element, leaves from many trees might help and the taller the tree the better. Aspen is a type of poplar sacred to Mercury, god of Airy matters, communication, commerce, etc., so this could be a good choice.
- Plant an acorn in the dark of the moon. As the tree grows, so will your bank balance. (Don't despair if it doesn't take root. Just try again.)
- Climb an almond tree for business success (careful, now!).
- Plant a gorse bush, for the gold flowers will attract like. This could work for many gold flowers, except that we are learning that proper money is Air and all you may get that's gold are a few coins.
- Carrying conkers is said to attract money.
- The 'money corner' is another area important in Feng Shui (please see references under 'Love Spells' to the subject of Feng Shui). As you enter your front door, your money corner is the area of your house or flat that lies furthest in front of you, to your left. If money is a problem, it is a good idea to attend to this area. Some people like to place there a round-leafed plant, and there is a specific plant you can buy, a type of succulent called a 'money plant'. These are now sold at inflated prices due to the popularity of Feng Shui! However, you do not need this specific plant. If you have no problems, leave this area alone. If you do, tidy it up, as a first move. Then you may like to experiment with small changes.

When we moved to the house we now occupy, I realized that our 'money corner' was actually out on the drive, as the house isn't evenly rectangular. After we moved we did have money problems. No, these were not the usual ones of an increased mortgage, because we knew that was to come and whilst not easy, we managed. What did happen was that many confusions arose regarding payments and bills. I did not receive payment for work I had done, not through anything nefarious, but through other circumstances. I placed a sticker, carefully chosen, at the appropriate window. Things improved, but not totally. To my horror my bank account became overdrawn by mistake and various other annoying things happened. So I made a special effort to get rid of an old garage door that was lying on the drive, in our money corner – this was in itself a magical act and, later that week, the door was duly carted off! Then I chose a special plant in a special pot, placing it on the drive to square it off, just in the money corner. Guess what! Within a fortnight my money bits were sorted and I even succeeded in getting the bank charges I had incurred for my involuntary overdraft revoked!

- One simple spell for money is to look at the new moon in the evening sky and to turn over the money in your pocket or purse. In this way you are making a connection between your money and the waxing moon. As the moon waxes, so will your money grow.

- In *The Crone's Book of Words* (see Further Reading) Valerie Wroth gives this spell:

A Hollyhock Spell, for Riches

The Hollyhock blooms in Summer
Its seeds in Autumn fall:
Then, in a folded paper,
Save them, gather them all –
The loose seeds,
The brown seeds,
The dry seeds,
The round seeds,
The seeds like tarnished pennies
That pay for the blossoms tall;
Bury their rusty treasure
Next to a southern wall –

> *With a mint coin,*
> *An ancient coin,*
> *A silver coin,*
> *A copper coin:*
> *By Spring your wealth shall measure*
> *Twelve times this sowing small.*

Sounds lovely, but it won't be megabucks, unless your 'ancient coin' is an antique!

A money ritual

A simple ritual for money is to construct your circle with the usual care. When prepared, write yourself a 'cheque' on a piece of blank paper. Visualize quite clearly how you will feel when you have this money, what you will do with it, including something you will do for others. Be filled with expectation. Know that this money is yours and on its way to you. (N.B. Theoretically it doesn't matter how large the 'cheque', for the principles are the same. In practice, you will have best conviction when working with a modest sum.)

Then you may consecrate this to all the four elements, but principally Earth for the benefits that will come, and Air for the Airy medium through which the money will arrive. Fire is relevant because it is connected to the realm of the possible and money is a key to this, while Water, too, is involved because of the peace of mind a healthy bank balance brings (I'm a great one for not leaving anyone out!). Annoint your cheque with oils of the correct correspondence: patchouli if you choose Earth, frankincense for Fire, ylang-ylang for Water, lavender for Air. Bearing in mind what we said earlier, lavender and Air could be the best choice. Then you can burn the cheque in your cauldron, if you have one. If you don't, an ashtray or similar container will do. The symbolism of money to burn could be a good one, but I don't like it. It could be better to place the cheque in your purse, or wherever you would usually put such things, and wait for the money to arrive.

Choice of correspondences, colours, etc., will depend on whether you decide money is Earth, Air or what. You may decide it is gold and ruled by the sun. However, the numbers of people who have done such spells and have been landed with sunflowers, goldfish or chocolate money wrapped in gold foil are too numerous to be encouraging. These days money is not gold, unless you are going to be content with a pile of coins, at best.

A final word on money – like attracts like. It is often said that the rich get richer and the poor get poorer. While there truly is plenty of unfairness in the world, it is utterly counter-productive to allow yourself to be consumed by resentment or overwhelmed by despair. 'I *never* get lucky, money never comes to me, I'll always be struggling,' etc. What a life script! Think rich, think fortunate, as much as you can. The same applies, of course, to almost anything. In the case of money, it helps to be literal about it and actually *have* some money, however little, rather than a mountain of debts. Avoid spending what you haven't got and always keep something in your account, however little, because it will attract more. I can't say why, but it does.

A spell to get rid of negativity

We all have things in our lives, personalities and habits that we want to be rid of. Remember, you are captain of your ship and you can be what you want to be, you only have to be clear and sure about this. This ritual can work for anything, but please don't use it for people as that would be most unethical. You will need to construct your circle, making sure it is tight, and ask for the special help of any elementals or deities that strike you as being the most potentially helpful to your purpose. Addictions such as smoking are the most difficult to banish, because they change you at a physical level and this level is the slowest to respond. So you come back to the everyday world, inwardly much strengthened, but with your body to battle with.

If you want to stop smoking, you need firstly to be totally, utterly committed. No 'Oh, well, perhaps it doesn't really matter. I enjoy it. Old Uncle Bill smoked for 70 years and died of old age at 96 . . .' Then you will also need other strategies in your life for coping with the 'smoking flashpoints' such as after a meal, or when you are out with friends, etc. Enlist others in your life to help you and ask friends and family not to smoke in front of you. Put all the money you have not spent on cigarettes in a special place and save for something really lovely. You need to plan very much on the physical level, as well as working on the magical.

When your circle is complete, sit in the centre with pen and paper and write down in detail what it is you wish to be rid of. If this is a recurring fear, such as getting an illness, losing your job, etc., imagine it in detail and write it down. Don't be afraid that imagining it will make it happen, because it is the repressed fears that maggot away in the unconscious and possess a power and reality. In any case, your circle is in place and you are not willing this to happen, after all, but much the reverse. You can put into the paper all your fear, disgust and revulsion at the habit, or whatever. Don't hold back. Remember, it is the habit you are hating, not yourself. You are lovely, beautiful, a channel of light, and you want this business out of your life. Stoke up your hatred and pour it into the paper. I do not recommend using any tools for this, such as your athame, because you will have to cleanse it afterwards. When you have finished, tear the paper into tiny pieces, with great relish and wrap the bits in toilet paper. Rinse your hands in consecrated water and cleanse yourself by passing incense through your aura. You may feel depleted. Move on to another gentle ritual, such as lighting a white candle and asking for the blessing of the Great Mother. My recommendation is to flush the paper firmly down the lavatory, after you have dispersed your circle.

Of course, you could burn it up in your cauldron, affirming that this transforms bad into good. However, the symbolism of the lavatory is my favourite. For simple matters you might choose not to write anything down, but simply to 'christen' some dried leaves in the name of the things you want out of your life and burn these or float them downstream later.

Spells for a new home

We covered a spell for a new home in our last Practice session. Another simple spell is to post yourself a postcard with a picture on it of the type of house you want. As with much that is magical, it is best to be as open as possible, not fixated upon one particular house.

A spell to retrieve a lost cat or dog

Dangle a string out of your window, or door, with a favourite toy belonging to the animal on the end and the name of the pet written on a piece of paper. If your pet does not have a toy, just the name will do. Calling your pet, slowly pull the string back in, with the paper at the end of it. Put string and paper somewhere safe, until you hear. Sadly, this does not guarantee that your pet will return safely. A friend of a friend who did this, quickly received word that her cat had been run over, several streets away. However, we all agree that the worst thing is 'not knowing'.

Moon spells

The moon is Mistress of Magic, ruling the instinctual tides as surely as she tugs at the seas. The hidden, the world of dreams and enchantment are all her province. The silver light of the moon reveals what is invisible by day. Naturally, the moon has a place in many folk spells. We have already encountered the power of the moon to increase the money in our pockets. Here are some more moon spells.

A spell to divine your true love

Wait for the first new moon in the New Year. Look at the moon and clasp your hands across your chest. Say three times:

> *New moon, new moon I pray thee*
> *Tell me this night who my true love will be.*

Then go to bed, without speaking another word to anyone. You will dream of the person you are going to marry.

A spell to rid a house of evil

Wait for the moon to be full. Peel nine lemons with your hands. Place the peels in a bucket of water, squeezing them, so that the oils are released. Affirm that the oils have the power to banish evil. Imagine them shimmering and glowing, casting out all that is negative. Hold this image in your mind as much as you can and use the lemon wash to scrub your floor, windows and doorknobs. As we tend to have lots of carpets in houses these days, I would recommend sprinkling the lemon water on the carpets. Pour some of the wash down each of your drains. Repeat this every full moon until the malign influences have gone.

Spells for good luck

- Simply blow three times at the new moon.
- Just make a wish. Before the year is out it will come true.
- When you see the new moon say nothing, but kiss the first person of the opposite sex that you meet. Then you will soon receive a gift.
- On the first day of the first new moon of the New Year, shut

your eyes, put your hand in your pocket and turn the smallest silver coin you have there, over. This will bring luck and prosperity for the coming year.

• Find soft ground on which to stand. Turn your money over, make your wish and turn around, three times.

The Moon is important to witches, for she personifies the three aspects of the Goddess in her three phases, waxing, full and waning. She also embodies the fourth mysterious and unseen aspect of the Dark Mother, when the moon is invisible, prior to the first appearance of the waxing crescent. Witches often plan spells and rituals according to the moon and celebrate her phases as part of attuning to the tides of nature and to a woman's body, for menstruation often follows the moon's phases. The moon affects men, too, and they are often more active at times of full moon. The moon's phases are given in many newspapers, calendars and diaries. Why not start your own moon diary and see how the phases of the moon affect you, or plan your spells and rituals according to the moon. Celebrate new or full moon by lighting candles, drinking wine, making love.

A spell to obtain a job

To get that special job you might like to do some cord magic. For this sort of success my personal choice would be a golden cord and it will need to be long enough to tie nine knots. It is best to do this in your properly formed circle, clearly visualizing yourself in the job. Take some time to imagine this, feel how good and successful you will be, imagine holding your letter of appointment in your hand. Hold the cord in your hand and, when you are ready, begin making the knots while saying this verse:

> *By charm of one, the spell's begun*
> *By charm of two, this shall come true,*
> *By charm of three, the spell shall be*

> *By charm of four, the open door,*
> *By charm of five, this spell's alive,*
> *By charm of six, the spell I fix,*
> *By charm of seven, earth and heaven,*
> *By charm of eight, the hand of fate,*
> *By charm of nine, the thing is mine!*

The final knot should tie the two ends, so the cord is in the shape of a circle. Place your knotted cord somewhere symbolically correct, such as around the base of your computer monitor, in your briefcase, or simply somewhere safe. When you get the job, burn the cord and make an offering of thanks.

This cord magic is highly adaptable and powerful, for it aids concentration and the rhythm of the chant injects it with power. You can use this spell for almost anything. I find that every time I use it I change the words somewhat – that doesn't matter. Keeping the rhythm going is the main thing.

A spell to bless and cleanse a new house

Even when buying a brand new house, there is bound to be a subtle atmosphere that you can sense, if you are sensitive. It is best to cleanse and protect your house on a psychic level, because the health and well-being of your family is dependent on there being a good atmosphere. Try to get into your new house or flat when it is empty, ahead of the removal porters. However, if this isn't possible, you can do the ritual after you have moved in and enlist sympathetic family members. Those who are prone to jeer can be sent out for an hour!

First visualize your protective circle, a sort of 'perspex bubble' that completely surrounds and covers your house. Go out and walk round it, if you wish. Obviously if you have a flat, this will not be so easy, but do whatever you need to, to reinforce your visualization, if you find it hard. Possibly sprinkle crumbs or flour. Define your space.

Now, starting in the topmost and furthest room or corner,

'sweep out' the house. If you have a traditional besom, so much the better, but if not, just wave a duster purposefully. As you sweep each room in turn, close the door behind you, going down the hall, down the stairs, doing the downstairs rooms (don't forget garage, large cupboards, etc.). Finally open the front door and sweep all the negative influences out. Ask the Goddess to disperse and neutralize them. Visualize them being sucked up, through the membrane of your circle, and dispersed in the atmosphere.

At this point you will need a tray, or a helper, to carry the bits, for you need a small dish of salt, a bowl of water, a joss stick or censer with lighted incense and a candle (white, preferably). A small Goddess figure, corn dolly, pentacle or similar is a good addition. Form a pentagram over the water before commencing. Starting where you began your cleansing, bless each room with all the elements, using words of your own choosing. You could simply say 'Be blessed by Earth' as you sprinkle the salt, 'Be blessed by Water' as you sprinkle water, 'Be blessed by Air' as you wave your censer and 'Be blessed by Fire' as you take your candle round the room. Actually, I don't feel happy making the salt and water do two jobs, one of blessing and one of purifying, so I take a 'working' bowl of water and a chalice, too, with a stone as my Earth representative, and the salt as a purifier alone. Finish with 'May the Goddess watch over this space' and form a pentagram over the window and one over the door. Some people also like to seal each door and window with salt and water.

Do this for each of the rooms, working downwards and outwards. When you have finished, place the four elements around you and say 'May this house be blessed' or other words that you choose. My friends, Jane Brideson, who illustrated this book, has these words:

> *May the winds of heaven consecrate your thoughts*
> *May the holy fire purify your heart*
> *May the living waters bless your every deed*

> *That you may cast away worry and doubt, and clearly*
> *understand Her will*
> *That you may burn out anger and pain, to know joy and*
> *wonder,*
> *That you may wash away all that is gross and impure,*
> *To receive with clean hands*
> *The blessing of the Goddess*

Sit with eyes closed for a moment, imagining your penta-grams at every door and window in turn – and don't forget the loft aperture. I like to place pentagrams over sinks and lavatories, too! Finally imagine a great, glowing pentagram over the roof of your house, feeling it bright and joyful. Affirm to yourself that this will be a safe, special place for you and your family, and add whatever affirmations you wish.

Give thanks, blow out the candle, put out the incense and scatter salt and water outside. Disperse your circle but retain the pentagram at the roof-top. Let go of the ritual, secure in your sense of accomplishment. Ground yourself. Celebrate.

Spells for safety on journeys

- A leaf from an ash tree is said to be protective and comfrey leaves are also good.
- Comfrey leaves in a suitcase are believed to prevent loss or theft.
- Consecrate some of either or both ash and comfrey leaves and place them in your luggage.

Spells for wart charming

Some people have a talent for getting rid of warts and can do it by a touch. If you haven't this skill, there are several things you can do.

- Cut a potato in half, rub half on the wart, place the two

halves back together and bury your 'wart' as the moon wanes.

- Get someone to buy your wart, which doesn't mean they get the affliction (but they might!).
- 'Leave' the wart, when you go on a trip. After you get back home, the wart will start to shrivel.
- Best of all, you can talk to it (nicely, of course) saying you thank it for visiting you, but would it now kindly depart.

A healing spell

Rub a green candle with oil of eucalyptus, saying:

> *Hale and hearty*
> *By my spell*
> *———————— [person's name]*
> *Is whole and well*

Visualize the person completely well, not 'getting better'. Light the candle and affirm to yourself that as the wax is transformed by flame so the illness is totally transformed to health. Let the candle burn out, or relight it daily, until it is burnt away.

Curses

If you have any sense, not to mention any humanity, you will not curse another person. Occult law states that any malevolence that you send out will return to you, some say threefold. It isn't worth it. In any case, nasty spells are a waste of energy, when you could be doing something to better your state. 'Live well is the best revenge.'

Most people are of the opinion that you cannot curse another person effectively without them knowing they have been cursed, and many voodoo and similar practices certainly seem to support this. When someone knows they have been 'cursed' their own subconscious turns traitor and falls in with the enemy and, through fear and underlying belief, the curse comes about.

However, I do not believe that someone always needs to know about a curse for it to be effective, for some people are vulnerable and some are good at cursing! The writer John Cowper Powys adopted what he called a 'neurotic benevolence' because the people he felt angry with seemed, all too often, to meet with extreme unpleasantness! Some people readily throw off their energies and do the sort of thing we aim for in a magic circle, unconsciously. This may appear an enviable talent, but it is difficult to control.

I do not mean to give the impression that we are all at the mercy of anyone or anything that seeks to work against us, because that is not so. We all have an etheric 'skin' that will fight off anything sent to harm. Regularly forming your magic circle will strengthen that skin. Healthy habits, regular meals and sleep, all the good old-fashioned things that Mother used to insist upon, do their bit also. And fresh air is wonderful. So please rest easy in the belief that malign influences will bounce off your aura and return to sender. As an ancient Chinese proverb says 'If a gift is given and not accepted, to whom, then, does it belong?'

It is most unusual to be really cursed. A majority of 'curses' are overactive imagination but, in a way, they amount to the same thing. If you feel you have been cursed, rituals will help. As you do your relaxation practice, imagine a protective egg-shape of blue light around you. This is your aura, a real, subtle but strong emanation of energy, visible to some occultists and having many layers. The 'working dimension' of your aura lies at about the extent of your arms, in an oval around your body. As you lie in a state of relaxation, imagine this egg-shape as a skin, similar to your physical skin, that allows impurities to escape but not to enter. Send all your doubt and fear out through this skin as grey vapour and then strengthen the skin, making it crackle with blue light. Anything that touches it will get 1,000 volts up their astral arm! If you are familiar with your etheric organs, your chakras, you will know how to raise power and circulate it via these. (There is a book devoted solely to the chakras in this series.)

As you progress through your day, do not try to tell yourself that you are 'imagining it'. Quite probably you are. However, it does not help to repress fears. Accept that you are afraid, hold the thought and throw it off. Strengthen your aura.

Valerie Worth, in *The Crone's Book of Words*, has a simple ritual to decrease another's power, to which I was introduced by witch friends some years ago, when I really did seem in danger of a physical kind, through obscene and threatening phone calls. Perform it in full circle, and enunciate the sounds clearly, reducing them to a whisper.

> *To shrink his lust*
> *And wither his dust,*
> *Call the first,*
> *Diminish the rest,*
> *Whisper the last:*

NORODAROGOR
RODAROGOR
DAROGOR
ROGOR
OGOR
OR

Other matters

Consecration

This is 'making sacred', a dedication to a power or deity, and we may like to perform this with the tools we use for spell-work, or for any special objects. Rituals for this can be complex or simple. You might simply hold the object and say 'I consecrate this to the Goddess'. You may form a pentagram over the object, pass it over the candle, through incense smoke, over water and against stone to consecrate by the elements. You may wish to leave it out in the light of the full moon.

Cleansing

A traditional way to cleanse magical instruments is to leave them in salt water for an hour. You could also hold the object in the running water of a stream. You may cleanse yourself, ritually, of whatever you wish to expunge, in a bath with salt or lavender oil added. Place white candles around you, for good measure.

Grounding

We have covered the methods for grounding yourself after rituals, but sometimes we need to find grounding in life, generally. The trauma of a broken relationship, betrayal, disappointment, and all manner of anxieties, can sever our connections with that which inwardly nourishes us, leaving us ill, jittery, weak and miserable. At such times it does help to concentrate on the basics, adopting what Jane Brideson calls the 'Granny Weatherwax' approach. If you find that you are prey to anxiety, relentlessly keep to your routines. If you have the energy, clean your living space, wash your clothes, clear out cupboards. If you do not, have a bath, clean your teeth, wash your hair, have regular meals even if you are so anxious that you eat only a bird's portion. You cannot control all the things that happen, so concentrate on the areas where you can be effectual, such as your bodily needs and your immediate environment. If you feel panic threatens to overwhelm you, wash your hands and rub in hand-cream, make a cup of tea, stamp your feet, breathe deliberately. Take Bach Flower Rescue Remedy straight on your tongue, or dissolve a few drops in water, ready to sip. Burn oils of cypress in an oil burner for solace and grounding, eucalyptus for healing. Many of these things may seem obvious, but they are what we usually do not do in a crisis. The same sort of conditions can apply when we discover we have a psychic gift, or start to perform magic, or embark on a spiritual path. By not eating, sleeping or looking after ourselves in the correct way, we are sending symbolic messages to our unconscious that all is not well, in addition to any actual problem. So remember that you are a child of the Earth Mother and care for yourself as She would. Times will improve.

Protection

The 'magic circle' confers protection and the more often you visualize it, the stronger and more readily created it becomes, so that you can feel protected whenever and wherever you are, by quickly 'throwing a circle' about yourself. A friend of mine who is striking in appearance managed to remain 'invisible' to someone she badly wished to avoid, by this simple expedient, even though he passed close by her. You may also have a protective 'cloak' that you visualize, or a 'power-field', generated by a special object you carry or piece of jewellery. Or you may have a power animal that you have encountered on shamanic journeys and for which you carry a symbol about you. Most of these devices can be reinforced by rituals when you form a ritual, magic circle.

Invocation

This is a term you may see used in reference to some rituals. It means 'calling up, inwardly'. In other words, what is invoked becomes an inward reality. When we call upon the four elemental Guardians we are 'invoking' them.

The gift

This lovely ritual was told to me by Jane Brideson, whose group perform it at certain times. It is a spell that is intended to open us to the abundance of the universe, not for a specific requirement. The gift may manifest as a physical object, an opportunity, a realization, connection, etc.

You will need a cord of appropriate colour, at least 1 metre (3 feet) long, depending where on the body it is to be worn: wrist, ankle, waist. Centre yourself and draw up energy. You may visualize this growing as a golden light in your solar plexus. Consecrate the cord by the power of the four elements. You will need to make nine knots, starting in the centre and alternating each side. As you are doing this visualize yourself receiving a gift, chanting 'The gift I desire is mine' nine times and ending 'As I wish, so will it be'. Charge with energy and tie on to your body. On each of the following nine days take off the cord and open one of the knots, keeping the centre knot until last. Keep the cord tied to your body and on the last day release the centre knot. As this knot is undone, release the spell by saying 'By the power of Air I release this spell' and blow on the cord. Then 'As I will, so will it be.' Bury the cord where it can rot naturally and return to the earth.

Watch out for your gift. It might not be what you expect and it might tell you something about yourself.

5

the round of
the seasons

Nature never did betray
The heart that loved her

Tintern Abbey, Wordsworth

Paganism, which is essentially about honouring the cycles of
Nature and the Great Feminine, observes and celebrates the
seasons. Usually this is organized around eight major festivals
or sabbats, but this does vary. For instance, in *West Country
Wicca* Rhiannon Ryall describes five festivals only: Lady Day
on 25 March, Beltane on 30 April, Summer Solstice on 21
June, Samhain (i.e. Hallowe'en) on 31 October and the Winter
Solstice on 21 December. This way may be more traditional
for the British Isles, for modern paganism incorporates ideas

from the continent, where the climate is milder and winter shorter. To the witches of the old West Country, the Lady slept during the dark months, which were given over to the guardianship of the Lord, who watches over the hibernating creatures and the frost-hardened earth.

The pagan 'year' is thought of as beginning at Samhain, which was the Celtic New Year (for to the Celts beginnings took place in darkness and, by the same token, day began at nightfall). Then comes Yule at the Winter Solstice, on or around 21 December, Imbolc at the start of February, Eostar/Spring Equinox at about 21 March, Beltane on 30 April, Midsummer on 22 June or thereabouts, Lammas/Lughnasadh on 30 July, Autumn Equinox on about 21 September, and so to Hallowe'en/ Samhain again. The 'story' behind this has variations, but goes something like this.

At Beltane the God has grown to young manhood and mates in the Greenwood with the young Goddess. Midsummer is a celebration of their union and the fruitfulness of the Goddess, but it has an underlying poignancy for, after this, darkness grows. The God begins to turn His face inwards. The God is often associated specifically with the sun which now begins to recede (although the sun is feminine in many cultures, including Celtic culture). The Goddess is closely associated with the land and She is seen to give birth at Lammas (which means Loaf Mass and is also called Lughnasadh, or Feast of Lugh, who was a god of brightness and creativity, possibly also a solar deity). At this time, midway between the hay and wheat harvests, fruitfulness is at its height, but it also marks the death of the Corn Spirit, so it is a funeral as well as a celebration. The Corn Spirit, or John Barleycorn, is also an aspect of the God, for the sun has come to earth in the soil. History shows that real monarchs were sometimes sacrificed, usually willingly, at this time.

And so to the Autumn Equinox, an eerie time, when light and dark are momentarily balanced, but the scales tip towards the growing shadows. Again fruitfulness is celebrated, the coming darkness honoured. The God departs to the Underworld, where He is enthroned at Samhain, and the Goddess reigns as Crone. Darkness holds sway in truth at Samhain, the beloved dead are remembered and issues of loss may be ritually observed. In modern times this is all symbolic, and Samhain is about coming to terms with things that may frighten us and with parts of ourselves that are hidden and 'shadowy', but in more ancient times the loss was real, in the old people and sickly folk who would probably not see the following spring and in the livestock that had to be culled.

Winter Solstice, for many, marks the rebirth of the sun-god, born of the Goddess, as the sun slowly begins to climb in the sky. Imbolc is a thoroughly feminine festival, special to the Goddess in Her form of Bride (pronounced 'Breed'), the Celtic goddess of poetry, smithcraft and creativity. At this time priestesses were initiated. Spring Equinox is principally a festival of the fertility of Nature, and so we return to Beltane and the young Goddess and God at the height of their vigour. Beltane is rightly a celebration of sexuality. Please note: while the Goddess gives birth, cyclically, to the God there isn't any incestuous element implicit, for She also gives birth to Herself, renewing Herself as the Spring approaches. The young Goddess and God meet as equals, innocent and wise.

The above is the general 'story' but there are many variations and there may be aspects of it that do not appeal. It is a way of relating to Nature, by which I do not mean that it is all 'pretend', but it is not 'true' in the way my keyboard is 'true'. Of course, the 'truth' of the seasonal cycle is in some ways more important, for it is about our essence, our Source, our place in the cosmos. The myth that we use to describe it is not fiction, but a way of embodying spiritual fact. If there are other myths that are truer for you, you will need to find them. However, I am using this general story as a background.

Rituals for the festivals

Pagan traditions worldwide honour the seasonal cycle in some form. The eight festivals here described are possibly a combination. Originally the Celtic festivals were four in number: Imbolc, Beltane, Lughnasadh and Samhain. They marked important points in the cycle for herding peoples. The solstices and equinoxes may be continental imports and are more linked to agrarian customs. The main festivals can and do span several days, and were no doubt not bound to a calendar but on observation of the earth. Solstices and equinoxes are astronomical events, marking the movement of the sun. They are astronomically exact at a certain time, although this can vary by a day or two from year to year. However, even in the case of the solstices and equinoxes, celebration does not have to take place on the exact day. Pagans in the Southern Hemisphere usually like to rotate the seasonal observances around the 'Wheel of the Year', celebrating Lughnasadh at the start of February, etc., although there are some who adhere to the traditions of their forebears and celebrate as if they were still in the British Isles. However, I and many others think that it is preferable to adopt the 'where you are' approach, for that is largely what paganism is about. If this is your first encounter with the idea of the Wheel of the Year, or if you are not familiar or attuned to it yet feel an interest, I would strongly suggest that you consult the books mentioned in Further Reading in order to feel a deep understanding and to make this a part of your life. Whoever you are, wherever you are, you may celebrate the seasons and the festivals in a way that appeals to you and enhances your sense of connectedness to the natural world.

Esoteric and exoteric

Pagan observance has two levels, the esoteric and the exoteric. Esoteric rituals are hidden and have inward significance. Often they are part of mystery cults, such as witchcraft, and are explored by initiates, to deepen their awareness. Here we shall be looking principally at some 'exoteric' or outward observances that you can use to celebrate with friends and family. Your enjoyment can only be heightened by an appreciation of the underlying meanings.

No book on ritual could possibly be complete without some suggestions for celebrating the seasons. However, here we do not have the space to examine the matter in depth, so this must simply be a 'taster'. Mostly, as stated, these are exoteric, and so no protective circle needs to be cast.

Imbolc

Let us begin, not with the Celts at Samhain, but at the time when most of us feel inspired to make 'new starts'. Tentatively, the light is growing and we see more of the bleached sky of winter. Snowdrops peep up and tiny lambs appear in the freezing fields. White and candles are things we associate with Imbolc, and the rather brittle light speaks of the sterner aspect of the Goddess as She encourages us to stretch ourselves, as She would Her newly initiated priestesses.

With Christmas and New Year over, many people begin to diet. Personally I am strongly against reducing diets, for if they are not well planned they deprive the body of essential nutrients and, in any case, they teach the body how to withstand famine – thus, in the long run, I observe regular dieting makes people fatter. Besides, reducing diets are miserable. However, we may like, at this time, to revamp our diet, making it less toxic, more pure, more filled with wholefoods and vitamins, kinder to the environment, and we may like to detox by fasting for short periods, taking only fluids. This can be turned in to a ritual occasion by doing it with a group of friends. A fresh exercise programme can be a similar idea. You may like to get together with a group of friends, each light a candle to your new venture and toast it with white wine.

If you feel moved to spring clean, either now or at the Spring Equinox, why not do this also with friends, getting together in a group and taking it in turns to clean each other's homes. Sweeping can be turned into a spell. The occasion could be sealed by taking a single large white candle from room to room and saying 'Welcome Spring'. If you are artistically or literarily minded, you may like to organize a poetry or craft evening, where like-minded friends can read out little snippets of their own or other people's creative writing, or you may like to sew a patchwork quilt for a charitable cause, as you sit together in a circle. You could select an appropriate theme for the conversation, for example 'creativity' and see what ensues. Remember, this is the Feast of the Poets, when the Goddess bestows and rewards creativity. Celebratory foods could be provided, keeping to the theme of white, and everyone could contribute a plate of food – some Caerphilly cheese with silver-skinned onions on sticks, small iced biscuits, vanilla ice-cream, lychees, natural yoghurt and milk puddings – use your imagination, and of course there is plenty of alcohol that is 'white'!

Spring equinox

Usually spring is visibly underway and the days longer. Now light and dark are in balance, but light is gaining. Easter, which always falls on the first Sunday after the first full moon after the Spring Equinox is only weeks away, at most. Easter is actually named after the Teutonic goddess Eostre, who was patroness of fertility and spring, and the custom of painting eggs arose in her honour. While children can be involved at Imbolc, at the Spring Equinox there is more for them to do. In my family we always hide eggs around the house, in locations of varying obscurity, in order to provide a challenge for every age group. Usually the challenge is too much for all of us, as the adults can't even remember where they are all hidden, or how many there are, and the last egg can be happened upon (or sat upon!) days later. This is a family 'ritual' for us and I always take photos of excited faces and figures teetering on the seats of chairs, groping for hidden goodies.

However, perhaps the best 'ritual' for this time of year is about planting something, from flower seeds to small trees. If you plant a tree as a group, tell everyone to bring a bit of soil from their own garden to bed it in. After it has been planted you could link hands and dance around the tree, or chant a short verse. How much of a formal ritual you wish to make this will depend on the participants. Another way of marking the Spring Equinox is to group together, in a way similar to Imbolc, and this time take it in turns to do everyone's garden, having a gardening party, followed by a supper, where, again, everyone brings something to eat. Green and yellow are colours I especially associate with this time. Why not decorate the table with primroses in pots (to be planted out later), light green candles and have a cake iced in yellow or orange at the centre as a symbol for the growing power of the sun?

Beltane

Beltane is the 'X-rated' adult festival, when sexuality and bodily joy are celebrated. Of course, this does not mean that children can't be involved and you may like to have a kids sleep-over party with giggles and midnight feasting. To the Celts this was the start of summer, so you can toast the final departure of winter as the sun sets on 30 April. Fill your house with flowers, go out and gather greenery from hedgerows and gardens – from anywhere where it is not threatened or in short supply. You could decorate a bush or small tree in your garden, hanging ribbons and sweets from its branches (as long as there are no lingering Spring gales) and dance around it, as a substitute for the traditional maypole. As you can imagine, lots of wine and a little staggering can make this hilarious. All the festivals, can, in a sense be considered Fire festivals, but this is especially so at Beltane, when the 'Bel-fire' was lit to herald the return of fertility and cattle were driven between two fires for purification. Couples can jump the Bel-fire, for heightened passion, *before* swigging the May wine, please!

However, adults may like to mark the sexual aspect of the festival, as it is a celebration of the union of Goddess and God and the generative forces of masculine and feminine, the Sacred Marriage. Old tradition was for young people to stay out all night in the greenwood, going 'a-maying' which was supposed to mean gathering hawthorn – unlucky if plucked before this day – but this often meant making love on a spring night, the so-called 'greenwood marriage'. So, if you are in a relationship, why not turn this into a sensual festival, with red or deep pink candles, massage oils and fine wine? Or go out for a meal, take a walk in the evening, make love under the stars, or by the light of the moon. Some prefer to celebrate the festivals, at the nearest full or dark moon, and so you may choose the first full moon in May to mark Beltane. If you are not in a relationship, you can set aside some time to indulge yourself, in any way you please. Have an aromatherapy massage, plan a meal of everything you find delicious, take a luxurious bath. Beltane is 'body-time'.

Midsummer

The solstices were often marked by alignments in ancient stone circles, and it is a good custom now to visit any ancient site to partake of the seasonal climax. Take a picnic and enjoy the longest day by playing sports or walking, far into the long evening. Midsummer can seem a kind of anticlimax, because it doesn't have the ambience of Beltane, or quite that air of excitement. Astronomically Midsummer is significant and you may like to head for a local high point, early in the morning, to watch the solstice sun bob up in the small hours.

This is a great time for large gatherings, barbecues and outdoor events. In the Northern Hemisphere, Midsummer marks the entry of the sun into the Water sign of Cancer and you could mark this by having beach parties, water fights, picnics by a lake, boat trips and similar. If you have like-minded friends, you may like to mark the fact that the light of the sun will now diminish by submerging a lighted orange candle in water to extinguish the flame. In the Southern Hemisphere, the sun enters Capricorn, at the Northern Hemisphere's Summer Solstice, and so, if you wish, you could snuff out your candle with soil or stone, as Capricorn is an Earth sign. Keep a few moments silence, then relight the candle to mark the recommencement of festivity. Roses are at their most vibrant at this season, so deck out your Midsummer table with fragrant bunches.

In *The Family Wicca Book* Ashleen O'Gaea describes the brilliant idea of the Summer Solstice tree, on which to hang tokens of joy, in a fashion paralleling that of the Christmas tree. The Summer Solstice tree is called a Sun Pole. Think about anything you have done or are doing that gives you pleasure and fulfilment and hang a symbol of it on the tree, a feather might mean freedom, a ring might mean relationship, a doll might mean motherhood. You can make your own mini Sun Pole if you are doing this alone, and it could be uplifting to the spirits to contemplate your decorated Pole, with all the symbols of joy upon it. Don't forget the small things. If your achievements are not spectacular, mark them, nonetheless.

Lughnasadh

This is an ambiguous festival. Everywhere is laden with fruitfulness, but while we celebrate the harvest we are also marking the fact that the year now noticeably declines. Already there are a few yellow leaves on the trees. The bright God of Nature is preparing His farewells.

With a few ears of wheat you can make your own 'corn dolly'

to enshrine the generative power of the Corn Spirit until next year. Your 'dolly' could just be a sheaf tied with red ribbon, or as complex as your artistic talents will allow. Make the 'dolly' a centrepiece on your Lammas supper table and light candles of honey-colour. A good way to mark this occasion simply is to acquire, or make if you are good with yeast, a spectacular loaf in the shape of a plait, garland or whatever, and turn the sharing of the loaf into a ritual. The rising of the yeast can be turned into a spell. Bury a little outside, as an offering, and in recognition of the death of the Corn Spirit.

This is a wake, as well as a celebration, but a wake can be hilarious, for departure into Otherworld is not only a sad occasion. As a group activity it is hard to beat a romp at a barn dance. Get together with like-minded friends and celebrate your creative gifts, for this is the festival of Lugh Longhand, the Irish master-craftsman god. In a sense this is a mirror image of Imbolc. Everyone should be encouraged to display what they can do, although shy and modest friends may need lots of encouragement. Recently at an astrological evening organized by my friend and colleague Graham Boston, we were given two minutes to enlarge upon the virtues of our sun-sign, with a partner. Just the good things, nothing negative at all. It was amazing how hard this was to do! As an exercise in self-esteem, at Lammas, why not do this with a friend, or in a group. Good friends can help you dig up more things about yourself and check you when you fall into self-deprecation. Sometimes, when we are really good at something, we hardly rate it as a skill because it comes easily, and friends may point this out. Then it is their turn. It's a good exercise in being positive about oneself. If you are alone try your best to do this for yourself.

Autumn equinox

Autumn is really in the air, now, but it may still be warm, mellow and misty. A beautiful time, but poignant, as we say a lingering farewell to the light and heat. The Autumn Equinox is suitably marked by gathering blackberries from the hedgerows, with friends, family or alone. There is so much symbolism here: the colour of the berries speaks of mourning and yet their metamorphosis in a delicious pie promises transformation; the natural surroundings and the lazy buzz of insects puts one right in touch with the seasonal tone; and the difficulty of getting at the prize fruit, pricking fingers and the like, has obvious meanings. Besides, it's good fun, always important at any festival.

The spirit of life sinks now, into the land once more, and the veil between this world and Otherworld is thin. If you have a garden or a patch of land that you wish to cultivate, adapt, clear, landscape or merely plant a few bushes in, this is a good time to commune with the spirits of the land, the faeries and devas that care for the earth on a subtle level. Magical expert Lionel Snell suggests that the best way to decide what to do with your garden is, in a sense, to ask it. To go out and sit in the space, encourage a drifty, dreamy consciousness in yourself and note what comes to mind, for the deva of the space will, in all probability, communicate with you. Autumn Equinox seems an excellent time to turn this into a small ritual, where you honour the four elements and directions and sit quietly in a space that you have made sacred, to see what comes to mind. Choose a soft, still evening, preferably when the moon is full, with candles of purple.

During the autumn, as a group, it is good at some point to take part in a charity scheme, of any sort, to raise money for those less fortunate, for famine victims and such like, to make this a 'harvest for the world'. You can go on a sponsored walk, in the cooling sunshine, organize or help at jumble and produce sales, or simply send a donation.

Samhain

This is the most controversial of festivals, because it explicitly honours darkness. Those who do not understand the pagan way feel that it encourages evil. However, pagans feel that it is healthier to give place and even honour to things we find fearful in the external world and reprehensible in ourselves and others, for, as C.G. Jung, the father of analytical psychology observed, 'nothing dies that is not lived out'. This is far from meaning that we have *carte blanche* to mug, steal, rape and murder, but it does mean making any such urges and anything allied to them conscious in ourselves, so we may be aware of our destructive impulses. Samhain rituals, such as trick-or-treat and the eerie pumpkin face are a way of doing this.

Samhain marked 'summer's end' to the Celts, but was also their New Year. We honour darkness, as a time of beginnings as well as endings, and the home of Mystery. This is the start of the story-telling season and an excellent way to mark it as a family is to tell ghost stories, by candlelight, or to tell a story in relays, where each person has two minutes in which to relate before the 'talking stick' passes on to the next person. It is fascinating how the scenario changes, according to the latest book someone has read, or the most recent film another has seen.

The English custom of burning a guy on a bonfire, linked to the English traitor Guy Fawkes, has older and sinister meanings connected to human sacrifice. I have always thought that the guy is a bit macabre, but kids love it, and I would suggest not waiting for 5 November but burning him at Samhain, and setting off the fireworks, too. Samhain was a primary 'Fire festival'. Dressing up is another way to mark the 'tricky' season, and the fun of apple-bobbing is also symbolically appropriate, for apples are an Underworld fruit, food of the gods and the dead. For a more serious ritual, as this is the feast of the Beloved Dead, you, and like-minded friends, may like to light candles to dear ones who have gone before, talk about them, laugh and cry too, and remember. Black candles are seasonal.

Yule

Yule comes three or four days before Christmas, on or around 22 December, when the sun 'stands still' in the sky. Perhaps the ancients watched in fear in case the wonderful sun might choose not to return. On Christmas Day, the return of the sun does at last become obvious, as it again begins to climb in the sky. The celebration of the birth of Christ was purposely set to coincide with the much more ancient festival of Yule, when the Sun God is reborn.

So many of the traditional things at Christmas are rituals, without us realizing it, and it can only add depth and enjoyment if we understand the symbolic meanings. The evergreen tree is symbolic of the enduring power of the Goddess, decorations of predominantly green and red are colours of life that is now returning, with the glitter of gold in especial honour of the sun. Actually such decorations may be as much a conjuration as a celebration, as if by symbolically depicting the sun's return, with bright colours, the God is tempted back. The gifts we give each other are gifts for the 'baby'.

Decorating the Yule tree is a ritual that can be done with the whole family (things can be rearranged more artistically later, when children have gone to bed!). Children usually make decorations at school or nursery, and these should be hung proudly as a measure of achievement. The theme is 'gifts'. Each person can choose an article to hang from the tree to celebrate a gift he or she has been given, or something they have to give, which may be even better. Articles can also be chosen in honour of a favourite Goddess, or God, or myth. For instance, some years ago I chose a golden horse, which was actually a roundabout horse, but it looked better when the baby had broken off the bottom part of the roundabout pole! For me this horse represented the myth of Rhiannon and Pwyll, from the Welsh story collection called the *Mabinogion*, and this was significant to me for a variety of reasons.

Holly and mistletoe also have special meanings in magic and tradition. Mistletoe is revered by the Druids as a powerful symbol of the 'entry into time' of the life-force. Mistle-berries are semen-white, and linked to fertility, while both holly and mistletoe are protective herbs. Holly King and Oak King are two aspects of the God, that battle at the Solstices. At Yule Oak King wins, while at Midsummer Holly King wins. Holly is the 'dark' aspect, oak is the 'light' but both are equally valuable and 'dark' does not mean evil. Mistletoe grown on the oak is most prized, and so in holly and mistletoe we have hints at an old tradition that is encoded in many tales, such as that of Gawain and the Green Knight. Ivy, too, is a seasonal plant and it was ivy leaves that were said to induce the ecstatic trance of the followers of Dionysus, the wine god. Ivy is holly's 'magical mate', worn by women, while holly is best carried by men. Yule garlands should have equal measures of each. So, when you hang your Yule wreath, you are honouring many traditions and deep inside the ritual meanings are registered. Even the circular shape of the wreath signifies the 'Wheel of the Year'. So as you perform all those Yuletide observances, realize their ritual significance to usher the return of the sun and enjoy them all the more! Candles of bright red or green are suitable now.

The moon

A shorter cycle of growth, maturation, decay, disappearance and transformation is performed for us by the moon, making change a part of our lives and teaching us, monthly, about renewal. Many things are governed by the moon, including the tides, menstruation, plant growth and births, for my midwife confirmed that she is busier at full moon and surgeons observe that the likelihood of heamorrhage is greater when the moon is full. When the full moon hangs high above, like a glistening pod about to burst, the atmosphere is highly charged and admissions to mental institutions increase, along with accidents and crime.

If we consciously and respectfully attune ourselves to these energies then we are less likely to be buffeted by them, more likely to make the best of our fluctuating rhythms. Men, too, have rhythms, but may need to be more diligent about observing them, not having a woman's more obvious cycle. The best way to start is by keeping a diary, over the space of three months at the least, noting how one's moods, health, energy levels and drives fluctuate in accordance with the moon. Some people will be at a peak at full moon, while others feel best at dark moon.

You can observe moon phases in a simple way, just by lighting a candle, or candles. You may prefer white candles. Some traditions link white to the waxing moon, red to full moon and black to waning/dark moon. These may be linked to three aspects of the Goddess, Maiden, Mother and Crone, but also we may consider a fourth aspect, of the Unseen Goddess, at dark moon. You can celebrate moon phases by toasting, with appropriate colours and types of wine, fruit juice or other drinks. If you have a family shrine you could place upon it representations of the current lunar phase, such as pictures, effigies or other articles. If you choose crystals, garnets might appeal for full moon, bloodstone for waning, onyx for dark moon, rose quartz or pearls for waxing. You might like to wear these at the appropriate time. You could choose to review life in rhythm with the moon, winding down, letting go, cleansing and retracting as the moon wanes, observing stillness when she is dark, stepping up the pace with the waxing moon and coming to climax of activity and vitality at full moon, and so to the downward cycle again. The purpose of marking lunar cycles is in order to be at peace with the surrounding world, to be grounded within oneself and one's environment and to adapt to cycles which are the basis of life. It is also poetical, beautiful and indeed magical. You will discover unknown depths if you go with the moon. Sit out in the light of the next full moon for ten minutes and see what comes into your mind.

Silver Lady, Queen of the Night, guide me around your
  circle
Where old becomes new, where new reveals the wisdom
  of ancient days
Where my dreams become real, and reality is revealed
As a moonlit dream

6

rites of
passage

At last he rose, and twitched his mantle blue:
Tomorrow to fresh woods, and pastures new

Lycidas, Milton

In life, the only thing that is constant is change, yet what the
great majority of us want is security and that applies in some
form or fashion even to the most adventurous souls. While we
may outwardly accept necessary changes, inwardly we may not
adapt to them. In some sense we may be living in the past,
however 'modern' we may be. Rites of passage help to ground
us in the new soil, to make changes and to ride with the evolu-
tion of life, to experience it as beautiful and meaningful even
when there is loss involved.

Birthday celebrations are a repeating 'rite of passage' into another year of life, and that is why we celebrate them, relentlessly. It is truly important to make a birthday a special occasion. Saying we're 'too old to bother' or 'don't buy me anything, I don't need it' can be a way of avoiding the acknowledgement of birthdays. Obviously, as we get older birthdays aren't going to be the riot of joy we experienced as children, but even, or perhaps especially, nonogenarians can celebrate another year of creative life. The birthday cake with its candles is a ritual. As children get older, consider them lighting the candles, one by one, counting as they go and saying 'Now I'm seven' (or whatever) as a climax. When the candles are blown out, encourage them to visualize how they would like the coming year to shape up, happy start at a new school, success at dance or piano class, lots of new friends, or whatever, and to release the candle energy with that in mind.

The three principal 'passages' in life are those of birth, marriage and death, and these are marked in our culture, although not always adequately. However, there are other passages, notably those of puberty, which are passed over, possibly with unpleasant consequences. 'Adolescent rebellion' may have not a little to do with the fact that the coming of adulthood is not recognized and affirmed, along with the increased responsibilities and independence entailed. Despite the fact that birth, marriage and death are observed ritually in our society, we may still wish for different, more personal or more pagan rites.

Birth

The purpose of a birth ceremony is to welcome new life and to acknowledge its sacred trust, and to give thanks and celebrate the joyful event. Pagan rituals do not commit the little one to any particular spiritual path, for that is a choice to be made when mature. This is a ritual to dedicate a new baby to the gods, adapted from a ceremony devised by Graham and Margaret Matthews and reproduced with their kind permission. You could use this ritual as a basis for constructing your own individual one, if you wish. Your wishes, and the people you have present, may incline you to something simpler, but this is beautiful.

Set your scene by placing two red and two white candles at each of the quarters and put your altar in the East, with salt, water, chalice, cakes, the candles and gifts for the baby upon it. The parents stand in the East, with a female and a male ritual leader (which would be High Priest and Priestess of a coven) standing in the North. The circle is formed by speaking

> *Joy, health, love and peace*
> *Be all here, in this place,*
> *We perform this rite*
> *To welcome the Light.*

Selected participants who will be the baby's guardians also stand at each of the quarters, representing the appropriate elements. Father and mother first speak the verse, then the male and female leader join in, then the Eastern representative joins in with the third repetition. At the end of the third repetition, the Eastern person joins left hand with the right hand of the next person, who then joins in the next repetition, linking then in the same way with the person on the left, who joins in as the verse is again said. This is continued until the circle is complete and the chanting is taken up by all, until the female leader declares 'Out'. Drumming can accompany the chant. (As a lot of energy may here be raised, I would suggest that it is focused upon some charitable cause, benefiting babies and children, as the energy is released.)

Now the Eastern person says, while facing East: 'Let this place be filled with the joyful Dawn Chorus, with the gentle lullaby of breeze-caressed leaves, with the drowsy humming of honey-bees, and the faerie song of the wind.'

The Southern representative faces South and says: 'Let this place be filled with crackling strength, with the warmth of golden, balmy days, the melody of crickets, the dozy scurrying of summer hedgerows; the scents of the noon-day sun.'

West says: 'Let this place be filled with cool, renewing waters; the rippling brook, the sighing sea; the slap of the leaping salmon; the haunting cry of the whale; the droplet on the still pool; the peace of evening.'

North says: 'Let this place be filled with the glittering light of the cold northern stars; with the enduring strength of the earth, our Mother; the tang of the heather and the silent breath of the distant mountains.'

Goddess and God are now called upon to be present and the male leader says: 'We are gathered in love to give thanks to the Gods for this new life, and to present _____ to the Beloved.' (N.B. You may here use the name by which your baby is to be generally known, or you may choose an 'inner name' from legend, mythology or the natural world, for example Bran, Etain, Rowan.)

The female leader says: 'Who stands guardian to this little one, to cherish her/him and help her/him grow in wisdom and love? Who will nurture the seed of promise, that s/he may in time unfold the full flower of her/his will?'

FATHER 'We, her/his parents accept responsibility in all matters for this little one, for her/his warmth, shelter, food and love.'
MOTHER 'We will take care of her/his being; physical, emotional, spiritual, to the utmost of our ability.'

The guardians in turn state their name and qualification and make an undertaking of their choice. Then the mother presents the baby to each of the quarters, starting at East, while the father speaks 'In the presence of the Gods I present _____ my beloved and sacred trust to the Guardians of the East' repeated at each of the quarters. Finishing at the North, the mother raises the child and says 'Lady, behold my Beloved, for whom I give thanks'. The father says the following verse, by Guy Ragland Philips:

Blessed Be
In your birthing,
Crying, feeding, learning
In your early years of earthing
Be Blessed.

Blessed Be
In your growing,
Walking, talking, knowing,
Goddess gifts bestowing,
Be Blessed.

Blessed Be
In joy and pain,
Crying, laughing, sun and rain,
Rainbow's arch, moon's wax and wane,
Be Blessed.

Blessed Be
In swallow's flight,
Valley's plunge from hill-top height,
Bluebells' ring in dappled light,
Be Blessed.

Blessed Be
In magic bowers.
Faery haunts, secret hours,
Child to youth, gently flower,
Be Blessed.

Blessed Be
In your heart's truth,
Passage of soul to age, from youth,
This sweet, strange journey upon earth,
Be Blessed.

Cakes and wine, mead or other drink are consecrated and passed round, moistening the baby's lips, and a toast is proposed to the baby. Gifts are also consecrated, with poems, blessings and other offerings from those present, as wished. The circle is closed and a feast follows.

Please note, the ritual as it stands is quite ceremonial and magical. Someone who knows what they are doing must take responsibility for the energy raised, for directing it, for closing the circle and for grounding everyone. Feasting is a good grounder in itself. Naturally, it is especially important that people should not feel spaced-out with a baby to look after!

Marriage

The purpose of a 'marriage' ceremony is to crystallize a commitment between two people, in whatever way they wish to make it, and to acknowledge and reinforce the fact that both are changed by the union. It is also a way to acknowledge the sacred gift of sexuality and its transformative and generative power (whether physical children are involved, or not).

After an ordinary ceremony at the local Register Office, my husband and I had our handfasting in the local wood, near our house. As there were people of all denominations and persuasions present we kept things low key, but they were naturally, noticeably pagan. 'Handfasting' is actually a term for a witch, or gypsy wedding, although as far as I know there aren't any authentic, traditional scripts. The place we chose, in beechwood, formed a natural 'circle' which I privately strengthened by visualization. We did not jump the broomstick, which is a traditional part of weddings, partly because I was pregnant and didn't fancy the sight of myself leaping about on father-in-law's video! However, I am delighted to have the short ceremony on film, as it was more atmospheric than I had appreciated at the time. Nor did we cut ourselves and mingle blood, because we thought some guests might be put off their food if we did, but these are elements you could include, if so wished, with appropriate safety considerations.

The ceremony was constructed with the minimum of props, as I had enough to think about on the day, but it could easily be made more complex, if you wish. Here is a simplified version of what we did.

One of the women present who had some experience and knowledge, asked for the presence of each of the elements, presenting my wedding garland to them and asking for their specific gifts on our union. Air for communication and exchange of ideas, Fire for warmth, passion and creativity, Water for companionship, understanding and mutual comfort and Earth for security, stability and prosperity. She then asked the Goddess and the God to be present. Then a male friend took over and, holding my wedding garland over each of us in turn, he said these words which we repeated after him, in turn. I went first. The words are:

'By seed and root, by bud and stem, by leaf and flower and fruit, and by life and love, in the name of the Great Goddess I, _____ take thee _____ to my hand, my heart and my spirit, at the setting of the sun and the rising of the stars.' These words were taken from *Eight Sabbats for Witches* by Janet and Stewart Farrar, and I felt they could hardly be improved.

My garland replaced upon my head, we exchanged rings and our friend continued: 'Let the sun, the moon and the stars, and our sisters, brothers and friends gathered here, be witness that _____ and _____ have been joined together in the sight of the Goddess and the God. May the God and Goddess bless them as we do ourselves. So may it be.'

Howard and I repeated 'So may it be' and thus was our little ceremony completed. Inwardly I gave thanks and closed down the circle, which of course had never been a formal circle. The whole thing took about ten minutes, but first there was the walk through the wood, absorbing the midsummer air, and a little explanation I gave to non-pagans who were there, encouraging 'mirth with reverence'. Afterwards came photos, discussion and the gentle walk back, for lots of refreshments. It was a lovely day and the beechwood was our cathedral.

Naturally you may adapt the above for gay weddings. There are many ways the ceremony could be lengthened: for instance, the couple could tread a spiral, into the centre; the group could dance, chant and play drums; you could choose to perform the ceremony by the light of the full moon, weather permitting; you may use extensive poetry to invoke Goddess and God, making the point that Man finds Goddess to some extent in the woman he loves, and vice versa (gay couples may feel they find all aspects of divinity in the beloved). The couple themselves can formally consecrate wine and refreshments. Actually this is unconsciously performed in the cutting of the cake, which the bride cuts while the groom guides her hand.

Requiem

The purpose of a requiem is to help us to let go of a person who has died, so we may adjust to the loss and accept that death is a part of life, meaning a return to Source, to the Goddess and to the tomb that is also womb. It also enables us to commune with the soul of the departed, to say our farewells for the last time upon this earth, to express feelings (which may be angry ones at being left) and to relive shared experiences. This ritual is an amalgam, from several quarters.

Cast your circle as usual. On your altar place white, red and black candles for the three aspects of the Goddess, as Maiden, Mother and Crone. Light also two purple candles for the Unseen Goddess and the God as Lord of the Underworld/ Upperworld, Osiris Risen. Here I emphasize the Goddess because it is to Her that we return, but you may wish for more emphasis upon the God, which is fine. A star map of the constellation Orion, which the Egyptians equated with Osiris, would be a beautiful touch and you could make this from a packet of luminous glow-stars. The God is the Guardian of the Shadowlands. Mythology here is somewhat mixed, as the Isles of the Blessed are in the West, while the eternal land of Osiris/Orien is in the sky, but you may not find this difficult, as the soul of your loved one now has the freedom of the universe.

Place a white candle in the West, for the deceased. Choose incense that includes myrrh and place sprigs of rosemary on the altar, for, as Ophelia tells us in *Hamlet* it is 'for remembrance'. Place flowers also upon the altar and possibly a photograph of the deceased. Lay a thread, in a spiral, around the centre of your circle.

Light the three Goddess candles, in turn, saying with the Maiden candle 'I honour the powers of the new, the fresh, the innocent'. Then with the red candle for the Mother 'I honour the powers of maturity, ripeness, creativity' and with the Crone candle 'I honour the powers of passage, dissolution, return to Source'. (If the deceased was old, you can include remarks about youth and age, but this is designed to honour three aspects of the life-force, whatever chronological age.)

Place the Crone candle in your cauldron, if you have one, or set it to join your Goddess and God candles, on the altar. Sit quietly for as long as you wish, communing with the dear departed, talking to her/him, reliving moments together, remembering, saying goodbye. When you are ready, gradually unwind the spiral cord, moving slowly round your circle, and saying, as you tread: 'I thank the Goddess and the God for the life of _____ S/He was _____ (here honour the departed in words of your choosing). May s/he pass peacefully through the Shadows and arrive in the Blessed Isles, in the eternal Summerland.'

Light your white candle in the West and say 'Farewell, _____ May your spirit rise free, wise and joyful, until you are ready once more to tread the spiral and take on the bonds of flesh. May you find peace and rest. Ever shall you live in the hearts and minds of those who love you. Ever shall you live in my heart, and my thoughts, but for now I bid you farewell, until we meet again, in the Light, on the other side of the Valley of Shadows.'

Contemplate again for as long as you wish. Burn the cord in your cauldron, or lay it aside to be burnt, or buried later. Move the Crone candle back in line with Maiden and Mother and move around your circle, celebrating the life-giving powers of each of the elements, in words of your choosing. Give thanks once more and consecrate wine in honour of the departed. If there is a group of your present, you may like to chant together 'We all come from the Goddess, and to Her we shall return, Like a drop of rain, flowing to the ocean, Isis, Astarte Diana, Hecate Demeter Kali, Inanna.' (This chant, written by Starhawk, can also be found on tape and may be available from the suppliers listed at the back of this book.)

Again, if you are in a group, you may wish to share stories, laugh and cry, in memory. Shut down your circle thoroughly, in the usual way.

If you have lost someone who is very dear to you, no ritual will enable you immediately to move on, because mourning will take time. An informal family or group ritual is simply to sit around and talk about the deceased. Someone should declare 'We are here to remember _____ in our own ways. We remember, because it is good to remember. We are here to feel because it is good to feel. Speak if you wish. Remain silent if you wish. Blessed Be.'

Have a 'talking stick' to pass around, but those who do not wish to speak may remain silent and this must be respected. The person who holds the stick speaks and is thoroughly listened to. This is important. It is important that feelings are heard and that the bereaved can cry and rage. Of course, in many families this is not acceptable because people find grief hard to cope with, preferring to repress, and thus find others' expressions of feelings uncomfortable. If you have a supportive group in which to express how you feel, this will be a great solace. Always close down the proceedings thoroughly and share food. Make another date for the next meeting, if this feels necessary. The purpose here is to work through, not to wallow. Groups develop their own dynamics and issues, and these can indeed give rise to problems of their own on occasion, but this is better than doing nothing. All group members need to be comfortable with extreme expressions of emotion, and empathic, but it will help if some are fairly detached and alive to the need to move on. Humour also is a great help – 'mirth with reverence'.

In many ways death is 'the last taboo'. Many people prefer not to speak of it or plan for it, but of all the things in life it is the one certainty. Some people believe that death really is the end of existence. Most pagans, however, do believe that life continues in some form, for energy is never destroyed, only transmuted. I believe that to regard the physical body as the sum total of our essence is nonsense. A movement is growing of those who plan for their own funeral. One person I know who died several years previously, expressed excitement at death and the forthcoming meeting with all the great minds who had gone before. 'Now I will really know all about it,' he said. When I die I want Bryan Adams singing '18 Till I Die' played very loudly at my funeral, and to be returned to nature with a tree planted over my remains.

Menarche

The onset of menstruation is a form of 'initiation' for young women, but it is not always marked in any way. I feel it is important to mark symbolically this passage, to celebrate it and to welcome the newly menstruating girl into the company of women. This may be done simply by the mother taking her daughter out for a meal and/or buying her a suitable gift. A more complex ritual could be composed on the following lines.

On the altar place two red and one white candles, with a large bouquet of red and white flowers. Place there a gift for the menstruating girl, wrapped in red, red wine and some sweets and pickles on a small plate. The circle should be cast before the young girl enters it and she should be welcomed into it by the other participants. Place the cauldron in the centre of the circle (any suitable bowl will do, if you have no cauldron) and dance around it, chanting, if you wish, 'She changes everything She touches, everything She touches changes'. Stop and direct the energy raised to a cause of the young woman's choosing. Then the young woman stands by the cauldron, facing North, while her mother, or other leading participant, takes one white flower from the altar and gives it to her saying 'This is the flower of innocence'. The young woman casts the flower into the cauldron. Then the older woman takes up a red flower, 'This is the flower of experience'. The young woman takes this flower also and puts it in the cauldron.

The young woman now lights a large red candle, placed in the cauldron, while the older one says 'We celebrate your power to bring forth new life. We celebrate the flow of blood, which is the blood of life. We welcome you to womanhood'. A pickle is now offered to the young woman, as a sign that life can be hard and bitter, followed by a sweet, for life's joy and sweetness. The red wine is consecrated and passed round and the young woman is given her gift, which should be suitably chosen, perhaps some red underwear, a red velvet pouch for carrying time-of-the-month necessities, a necklace of rubies or garnets, or similar. Some informal womanly talk and advice may follow. In time, close the circle and have a celebratory meal.

Menopause

Women in increasing numbers are recognizing the need to adjust to the menopause in a meaningful way, discovering its positive and creative aspects, as well as accepting the loss of childbearing potential. Here is a shortened version of a ritual given by Nancy Brady Cunningham in *I Am Woman By Rite* (see Further Reading) upon which I could not improve. It is intended as a solitary ritual, but there should be no difficulty involving a group, if so wished.

At dusk the woman carries an egg into her garden, or secluded woodland. (N.B. The ground must be soft enough to be penetrated by a small shovel.) She sits and meditates, and maybe she takes up a soft chant, simply of the word 'Changing'. In time she lights two candles, propped in the earth, contemplating the changes that have come upon her. Now she cannot have children, but there are many things she can do, now better than before.

She takes up the egg and, using a marker pen, writes on it the name of a creative project that she wishes to complete, such as writing a book, learning to paint or play an instrument, or whatever. Now she digs a small hole near the candles and cracks the egg into it, dropping the shells in, over the white and yoke. She mixes this with the earth, in a circular motion, visualizing the successful completion of her project. Every end is a beginning. Putting her hands into the soil, she buries her egg and places over it a stone, to mark her new status as Wise Crone.

Affirming that she will keep her creative channels open, she ends her ceremony by placing her hands flat on the earth, as a grounding. Now a new phase has been ushered in.

Men's rituals

In coven and cathedral, women tend to outnumber men by two or three to one. I am not sure what the reason for this may be, but I suspect it has to do with the fact that women tend to be closer to the pulse of life than men, and thus aware of the need for rituals. Women also bond more naturally and less self-consciously, while men are more competitive and more afraid of appearing weak or foolish. This, however, is changing fast. Increasingly men are looking to find connection to their spiritual and their sensitive side, and to heal so many of the rifts and wounds experienced in our culture, by performance of ritual.

The men I have consulted agree with me that the masculine psyche likes a challenge, something to do and complete, and men are often more comfortable actually doing something together – which may be arduous – than sitting around chanting and lighting candles. One example of a masculine 'ritual' consists of walking a sacred path, alone or with company, as an act of return to Nature, of worship and of bonding. Patrick Corbett, who originated this idea, regularly walks the Ridgeway footpath, by night, with a friend. The Ridgeway is an ancient track, starting in Hertfordshire, at Ivinghoe Beacon, passing near Wayland's Smithy (close to the Uffington White Horse in Oxfordshire) and ending at Avebury in Wiltshire. (This 96-mile track is believed to be the oldest in Europe.) Suitable for men in our culture, this is a type of vision quest. The traditional Vision Quest of the Native Americans involves being alone with Nature, as a rite of puberty. This is approached by fasting and sweat-lodge, and is too taxing to be undertaken by most people in our culture. However, safer forms of vision quest may be undertaken, with the guardianship of more experienced men.

A further example of this is given by James Hunt, who attended Spirit Horse Camp in Wales, where the participant goes down a mine-shaft. The shaft is pitch-black and horizontal, going on for ages and ages, and there is water on the floor. Those who enter have no idea what will happen. What transpires is unforgettable, but those who have experienced it say no more! 'If you undertake this you feel you've really done something,' James told me.

A men's ritual arose spontaneously at a men's camp, attended by James. Here there were two tepees, housing eight men.

Some of the men felt strongly that they wished to undergo initiation of some sort, having, they felt, missed out on a stage as they approached adulthood. The other men took on the role of Elders. A circle of stones was created and smudged, which means that a smudge-stick made up from sage and sweet-grass, or similar, was lit as incense and used to purify and consecrate the space. The Elders then planned the rituals, beginning in the circle, leading the participants around the woods and streams, naked at times, taking in the essence of the elements in movement and action. The Water element, for instance, would be sharply experienced by leaping naked into a stream. (From a woman's perspective, I wonder if that is a metaphor for how the emotional realm, as represented by water, impinges upon men, rather as an overwhelming shock, whereas to women it is more like home, and more gentle.)

After these experiences, those seeking initiation were left apart while the Elders took up positions in the tepee. They were then invited in, one at a time and asked what they had come for. They were given a symbol, metaphor or story where the answer would appear. After this they were led out and passed through something that represented their initiation, a type of archway made of flowers and boughs, and welcomed into the Circle of Elders.

It should be noted from the above that while these being initiated felt they needed it, and those bestowing the initiation were able to give something, the true initiation came from within the seekers and was not bestowed by those organizing the ceremony, only facilitated by them. So while some experience in these matters is invaluable, the presence of true 'tribal elders' is not essential – indeed, there is a dearth of these available to us! All that is necessary is sincere and trustworthy men, of good intent. However, if you are young and/or inexperienced, always choose companions for such ventures with great care.

The King

Another ritual mainly for men has been given to me by James Hunt. In this ceremony, each person takes it in turn to be king, on an improvised throne, made of colourful cushions and decked symbolically, perhaps with gold cloth, rocks from the garden, flowers and other decorations. Each person takes it in turn to be 'King' while others in the group take on supporting roles, such as Gatekeeper. While the space is being set, the King waits outside to be ushered in by the Gatekeeper when all is ready. Another person then places a 'magic cloak' around the King who takes his place on the throne. Amid humming and chanting, the King is offered three gifts, a flower (of life) some water and a poem. All those taking part sing a beautiful lullaby while the King is given lots of eye-contact and attention. For those doing this there is a wonderful feeling of giving. Being King, James describes, is a really interesting and revealing experience, because it shows how it feels to receive respect – something that is quite rare in our culture. Having this experience clarifies one's sense of direction, possibly awakening a realization of the importance of respect and therefore a greater focus upon meriting it and achieving it. A ritual like this can be a vehicle for growth.

Practice

Only you can decide if there are passages in your life that need to be marked by ritual, or transitions that you have not fully completed, for absence of this. It is not too late. Even if you were married ten years ago in a Register Office, you may celebrate anew your handfasting. The birth ceremony can be adapted for older children and you may seek initiation at any age. Take time to decide what you wish to mark in your ceremony and draw from the above to construct your own, if you wish.

7

superstitions

Superstition is the religion of feeble minds

Reflections on the Revolution in France, Edmund Burke

In a sense superstitious observances are a type of spell, usually a small ritual to ward off harm, or a belief that something can cause ill luck, or good luck, due to some strange power it exerts. Common superstitions can often be traced back to the same symbolic roots as spells. Many historians believe that cultures in the Stone Age and Bronze Age were matriarchal, or at least matrifocal, with emphasis upon the Goddess and her many different forms. In these cultures women had considerable power and may have been dominant. Goddess worship is different from worship of a patriarchal God in many respects.

The Goddess isn't 'God in drag'. True Goddess worship departs from hierarchical models and has little in the way of dogma. It encourages personal, inward revelation rather than adherence to strict observances and laws, and is a way of the instinct and the heart, rather than the mind. The ancient Goddess worship is believed to underpin much of present-day paganism, and to have been present, to some extent, in many cultures at the point when they were taken over by Christianity. The Celts are an example. As the 'Gods of the Old Religion became the devils of the New' many pagan beliefs, customs and symbols became evil, or 'unlucky' and this underlies many superstitions.

In *Cities of Dreams: When Women Ruled the Earth* (Aulis, 1995), Stan Gooch puts forward a more radical, but similar, theory. He argues convincingly that the Neanderthal had a flourishing civilization, that was nocturnal, women-centred and deeply magical. The Neanderthal had brains much larger than our own, with a 'bun' at the back housing their enlarged cerebellum, home of 'psychic' powers. Far from being brutish, they had a highly developed community, caring for their sick and old (as has been suggested by the discovery of herbs in ancient burial sites) and deeply infused with spiritual and religious observance. Gooch argues that Neanderthal peoples were not wiped out, but actually were conquered by Cro-Magnon man, who interbred with them, wanting yet fearing the Neanderthal magic. Much that is despised, feared or at least regarded with suspicion by our modern culture can, according to Gooch, be traced back to what was once powerful and revered in a worldwide Neanderthal kingdom. Here follows a selection of popular superstitions, with interpretations, some of which link with the Neanderthal theory.

Thirteen

'Unlucky for some' this number is so feared that it is sometimes passed over altogether in house numbers, with progress being made straight from 12 to 14 – as if you can get round it that easily! The fear of 13, in all probability, derives from the fact that it is a lunar number, connected to the movements of the moon. In *The White Goddess* Robert Graves develops the notion of 'lunar knowledge' as opposed to 'solar knowledge'. Lunar knowledge is that of the instincts, wordless, incommunicable, subconscious and yet extremely compelling. It is 'knowing in the blood', feeling and sensing. Under its umbrella come all the psychic gifts and, of course, witchcraft and indeed worship of the Goddess. The moon makes 13 rounds of the zodiac to a single circuit of the sun and, at one time, calendars were probably moon-based. The choice of a 12-month year as opposed to a 13-month year shows a clear movement away from lunar respect and awareness towards solar consciousness which is that of the rational, logical mind. This 'calendrical battle' is symbolically depicted in many stories, for instance where the thirteenth fairy is snubbed and wreaks revenge, in 'Sleeping Beauty'. Many epics conceal a hidden 13, for example Arthur and his 12 knights of the Round Table, and Christ with his 12 apostles. In such tales the thirteenth is both a sacrifice, and a redeemer. Hard choices have had to be made to construct our calendar, resulting in 12 months of varying lengths that do not make sense. Why not divide by 13? This would result, in a non-leap year, in 13 months of 28 days each, with one intercalary day. Quite neat. But 12 is a rounder number, more easily divisible, and thus more attractive to the 'rational' mind. Neanderthal, with their lunar emphasis, would no doubt have valued the number 13. Witches covens, perhaps for similar reasons, are believed traditionally to have contained 13 individuals (although these days that is rarely found).

Don't walk under a ladder

In walking under a ladder you are violating a triangular space. Magicians may construct a triangle outside their working circle into which demons and spirits can be safely evoked. The triangle is a symbol of the Trinity. We may think of this as Father, Son and Holy Spirit, but, more anciently, this 'trinity' is the Triple Goddess, Maiden, Mother and Crone, shown as waxing, full and waning moon (lunar symbolism again). The triangle is the simplest shape that can be constructed two-dimensionally. A triangle with apex pointing upwards means the element of Fire and the masculine; pointing downwards, like a chalice, it means Water and the feminine. A triangle is sacred space. Enter with care!

Throw salt over your shoulder

If you spill some salt, throw a pinch of salt over your left shoulder, to prevent bad luck. Well, in these days of refrigerators we don't respect salt for the preservative qualities that once gave it value, but salt was once a precious substance. However, there is more to the value of salt than the culinary. Salt is sacred to Aphrodite, goddess of love and passion. Aphrodite, in her more ancient aspect, was a goddess from the Middle East, a Creatrix of wild and awesome power. To the Greeks she was 'foam born' rising from the salty waves, where fell the castrated genitals of the titan Cronus, and gradually she became a creature of the boudoir, where her original domain had been forest, shore and hillside. Salt is associated with the element of Earth (heard the expression 'salt of the earth'?) and is used magically for cleansing and purifying. When we throw salt over our shoulder, we are making an offering to Aphrodite. It is wise never to anger the goddess.

Left hand

Thankfully the Victorian neurosis-inducing practice of trying to eradicate left-handedness has vanished, with left-handed people now being catered for in manufactured instruments. Stan Gooch, in *Cities of Dreams: When Women Ruled the Earth*, makes a case for Neanderthal people having been predominantly left-handed. The left side of the brain is the 'rational' half and this is connected to the right side of the body. So the left side, connected to the 'right brain' is less well co-ordinated and more instinctual. Some people are able to paint or write things with their left hand that seem to come from 'somewhere else' which they cannot manage with the right hand, and often psychic exercises such as psychometry are best carried out with the left hand. In left-handed people, this is reversed, and it is the right brain that is the logical hemisphere. However, the symbolism of the left being connected to the instinctual, pattern-perceiving side of the brain is deeply ingrained and, by association, the left is dark, magical and irrational. People these days are sometimes quite proud of being left-handed, but this is a recent innovation. The Latin for left is *sinister*. Need I say more?

If you see a hearse, cross your fingers . . .

Seeing a hearse is bad luck, so cross your fingers until you get the okay by seeing a four-legged animal, when you can relax! When driving, the dangers of this could result in a self-fulfilling prophecy! Obviously a hearse means death to this material world. Crossing your fingers relates not merely to the cross of Christ, but to the older equal-armed cross, of the four cardinal directions, four elements, etc. Thus, by crossing your fingers you are affirming that you are grounded in the here and now. An animal with four legs, one for each of the elements/directions, etc. confirms and earths this, so you can let go and relax, confident that the end is not yet nigh . . .

Good things come in threes, third time never like the rest, etc.

Many people consider three to be lucky. This has to do with the symbolism of the triangle, encountered above, with the ladder. In number symbolism, three is a creative number, relating to Mother, Father, Child, so there is a completion and balance about three, as if the 'run' is not complete until the number three has arrived. Accidents also are said to come in threes.

If two pour from the same pot, an unwanted baby will arrive

I must confess that at our family breakfast on Sundays I do insist that only one of us pours from the same pot! Could this be because I have two teenagers, and unwanted babies are to be feared? Not really. For me the symbolism of the pot is again about creativity. The older version of the teapot is the cauldron, presided over by the Welsh goddess Cerridwen and conferring magical powers. Story tells how Cerridwen brewed a magical potion for her son, but some of the liquid spilt on to the finger of Gwion, a little boy she had left to stir it. Naturally enough, he sucked his scalded finger and inadvertently acquired all the gifts of the cauldron, one of which was the foresight to know how angry the goddess would be on her return. He fled, but she sensed immediately what was happening and ran after him. There followed a long shape-changing chase, symbolic of many shamanic journeys, entering into the soul and spirit of animal forms, until eventually Gwion turned himself into a grain of wheat. Cerridwen became a hen and ate him, nine months later giving birth to the famed bard Taliesin. This Celtic tale shows the terrifying aspect of the goddess as muse, inspiratrice and initiator. I suppose the underlying meaning here is that the unauthorized drops from the pot are the ones with the most potential.

Spiders and snakes

Many people are plain terrified of these creatures, in a way that goes beyond superstition. Stan Gooch says that these creatures were sacred to Neanderthal as being some of few species where the female is larger than the male. Actually the serpent represents, in its spiralling shape, a passage into and out of the manifest world, and is a symbol of regeneration and primitive power, associated with the Goddess. Grandma Spider is Creatrix, in some creation myths, spinning the cosmic web. Neither of these creatures are lovers of the light and bright. Spiders scuttle from shadow to shadow and snakes lurk in long grass, so both have links with darkness and therefore with the unconscious. But remember

> *If you wish to live and thrive*
> *Let a spider run, alive.*

Magpies

Many people will be familiar with the rhyme:

> *One for sorrow, Two for joy, Three for a girl, Four for a boy,*
> *Five for silver, Six for gold, Seven for a secret, never been told.*

This is probably a fragmentary survival from divining by the flight of birds, practised by the Druids and others. When this is analyzed, it has nothing to do with the birds somehow 'knowing' anything, but much more to do with the mind of the diviner reaching out into the world and finding it reflects her/his unconscious knowledge (for somewhere, somehow, inside us, there is a part that 'knows all' and we strain to hear its voices). Magpies are related to crows, which were linked to the Morrigan, fearsome Irish goddess of war and death, and as such they have a sinister feel. However, they are also beautiful birds. The rhyme has obvious number symbolism, which we have covered elsewhere in the section on magical correspondences, although not all seems to 'fit'. One may be sorrowful because it relates to being solitary, or because the association with the Morrigan is unalleviated by 'safety in numbers'. Two is 'joyful' because, as anyone who has read *Winnie the Pooh* knows, 'It's much more fun for two'. Why three means a girl and four a boy I am not sure, because odd numbers are considered 'masculine' and even ones 'feminine'. Perhaps this means three is a gift for a girl (as in finding her masculine match)? Five may refer to the pentagram, used in 'lunar' magic and therefore associated with the metal silver, sacred to the moon. However, this is a 'mixed' rhyme, if these associations are correct, for we now move to the ancient Jewish mystical doctrine of the Qabalah to link six with the sun and, therefore, gold. Finally, seven is the easiest, for it is linked to the moon, to magic, and profound study.

Four leafed clover

This is lucky because it symbolizes a balance of the four elements.

Wishing wells

Water is a transformative, life-giving element that is often especially associated with the Goddess, as Water is regarded as a feminine element. We all float in the waters of amniotic fluid, before birth. A well or pool is obviously symbolic of the womb or the chalice, and so when we throw a penny in a wishing well, we are making a symbolic offering. We are also, in effect, saying that we respect powers other than those of logic and reason, and putting our money where our mouth is – a strong message to the subconscious mind that may, indeed, be 'lucky'.

Black cats

Considered both lucky and unlucky, this is probably a throw-back to the days when cats were believed to be witches' familiars, or shape-shifted witches themselves. As Egyptian Bast, the cat is a Goddess form, or totem. Black has been linked to evil, but relates to 'lunar knowledge'.

Horseshoes

Upright, as a cup, horseshoes relate to the chalice, symbol of the Goddess, holding luck within. Horseshoes could be hung upsidedown only over the forge, spilling the force into the trans-formative metalwork of the blacksmith, which was considered magical.

Practice

These are just a few superstitious beliefs and it is not hard to track down their meaning in terms of magic and Goddess-values. Indeed, many of the things we deem 'unlucky' are more likely to be 'lucky' if we are inclined to the Old Ways. Think about any superstitions or beliefs about luck with which you are familiar and your own feelings about them. Do you think they may have a basis in older pagan beliefs? And do they feel lucky, or unlucky, to you?

further reading
and resources

The Mobius Guide to Witchcraft by Teresa Moorey.

The Wheel of the Year: Myth and Magic Through the Seasons (1997) by Teresa Moorey and Jane Brideson.

I Am Woman By Rite by Nancy Brady Cunningham, published by Weiser, 1995.

Eight Sabbats for Witches (1989) and *Spells and How They Work* (1990) by Janet and Stewart Farrar, both published by Hale.

The Pagan Family by Ceisiwr Serith, published by Llewellyn, 1994.

The Family Wicca Book by Ashleen O'Gaea, published by Llewellyn, 1998.

West Country Wicca by Rhiannon Ryall, published by Capall Bann, 1993.

The Lunar Almanac by Rosemary Ellen Guiley, published by Piatkus, 1991.

The Enchanted Forest by Yvonne Aburrow, published by Capall Bann, 1993.

The Crone's Book of Words by Valerie Worth, published by Llewellyn, 1971.

The Complete Book of Incense, Oils and Brews by Scott Cunningham, published by Llewellyn, 1991.

Experimental Magic by J. H. Brennan, published by Aquarian, 1978.

Suppliers

The Sorcerer's Apprentice, incense ingredients and occult equipment, worldwide mail-order. 6–8 Burley Lodge Road, Leeds, LS6 1QP, UK. Tel: (0)1113 245 1309. Send two first-class stamps (or International Reply Coupons) for complete list.

Starchild, worldwide mail-order and shop. Incense ingredients and other products. The Courtyard, 2–4 High Street, Glastonbury, Somerset BA6 9DU, UK. Tel: (0) 1458 834663. £1.50 for catalogue, which includes magical information.

Enchantments, worldwide mail-order. Catalogue $3.00 USA, $5.00 elsewhere, US money orders only. Herbs, incense, books, magical apothecary, tarot readings and much more. 341 East 9th Street (between 1st & 2nd Avenue), New York, NY 10003, USA. Tel: 212 228 4394.

Eye of the Cat, worldwide mail-order. Herb and Hermetic Catalogues $10 each. $5 refund on first order. Incense, statues, books, jewellery and more. 3314 E Broadway, Long Beach, CA 90803, USA. Tel: 310 438 3569.

Mystery's, mail-order herbs and oils for magic and ritual. 386 Darling Street, Balmain, NSW 2041, Australia.